IMPOSSIBLE TO IMAGINE

Printed and bound by Lightning Source UK, Milton Keynes

Published by Crossbridge Books
Berrow Green,
Martley WR6 6PL UK
Tel: +44 (0)1886 821128

© Crossbridge Books

First published 2010

ISBN 978 0 9561787 5 6

British Library cataloguing in Publication Data.
A catalogue record for this book is available
from the British Library.

BIBLICAL QUOTATIONS
are taken, unless otherwise indicated, from the
HOLY BIBLE, NEW INTERNATIONAL VERSION
Copyright © 1973, 1978, 1984 by
International Bible Society.
Used with permission.
Other versions: King James (1611) Version (KJV)
New King James Version (NKJV)
The Living Bible (TLB)

IMPOSSIBLE TO IMAGINE

Ruth Parry

with *Gill Shiels*

CROSSBRIDGE BOOKS

Acknowledgements

Grateful thanks to Ann McDonald and Ron Evans for typing up the book and putting it on to computer. Thanks also to those who checked through certain chapters: Sarah Carter for looking at the chapters on China, and Barbara Cross and Brenda Hawksley for looking at the chapters on Congo.

Thank you to my husband for supporting me in bringing this book up to date and getting it published. And thank you to Crossbridge Books for recognising the value of the book's challenges and publishing it.

A very big thank you must go to my niece Lisa Lewelling, who proofread the typescript and suggested grammatical changes — thanks Lisa.

Finally and most importantly, thanks and worship must go to the Lord for His faithfulness and for the wonderful plan He has for anyone who will follow Him, as is clearly demonstrated in this book.

"No eye has seen, no ear has heard, and no mind has imagined what God has prepared for those who love him." (1 Cor 2:9)

In other words, impossible to imagine.

Gill Shiels

Contents

The 'Dove-cote' – our tiny home on the mountain in Tibet

1

The Beginnings

My heart was pounding.

This was never going to work and we would look so foolish. Our unexpected visitors sat with us at the dinner table, smiling and chatting and looking forward to a good meat and veg dinner. But I knew the size of the roast and I knew it was hardly enough to feed us, let alone the visitors.

I knew Mother would pray over it and trust God to multiply it — and in times past God had done just that, but I just knew it wasn't going to happen this time. Well, Mum and Dad would cope with that, but I would be so terribly embarrassed.

Mum came in with the first two plates of food and gave them to the visitors. I looked furtively and there was plenty on the plate. 'Well, it's me that's going to do without then', I thought.

Plate after plate came to the table until we all

had a plate of a good-sized dinner. With a deep sigh of relief and no small sense of awe, I knew God had done it again. He had answered Mother's faith and multiplied the food on the plates.

This was normal for us children. We saw God work in miraculous ways and learned quite early in life the value of prayer and childlike faith, whether it was meat on the table or milk continuing to pour from an almost empty jug. In such an atmosphere of practical Christian living I grew up and so learned to prove Him for myself.

We lived in an ordinary terrace brick house, one of twenty-eight of uniform monotony. Each backyard fitted closely to the next and was guarded jealously for that degree of privacy that was necessary. No one boasted a garden. In those sunless, smoke-laden surroundings I doubt whether a blade of grass would have taken root. The yards were so cramped that one shed occupied most of the space, leaving just enough room for free passage to and from the "little house" in the corner. Indoor sanitation was still beyond the reach of ordinary folk.

There were five of us children and consequently our house always seemed to be overcrowded. Visitors dropped in frequently for Mother's hot-pot suppers, which were a constant attraction. In spite of little money and plenty of cares and anxieties, we were a happy family, blessed with a Godly father and mother. Sunless surroundings maybe, but we children nevertheless led very sunny lives.

Mother was both thrifty and ingenious, producing tasty meals out of very little. Her clever needlework kept us three girls neatly dressed, though not always in the height of fashion.

2

In those days of slump following the First World War work was scarce and money even more so, consequently Mother was obliged to put her hand to all kinds of jobs in order to make ends meet. Her meat and potato pies, which she made and sold every day were renowned, and we children, coming from school with keen appetites, would find them sharpened by the delicious aromas which greeted us.

Father was a typical family man, delighting in his home and family. One of my earliest recollections is of the happy hour preceding bedtime when he would sit in the old rocking chair, my sister on one knee, myself on the other and my eldest brother standing behind, while he told us, with vivid and dramatic actions, the stories of the Bible.

Our favourite was of Jonah, and we insisted on hearing this every night, hanging breathlessly on his every word and wriggling with excitement as he described the storm at sea. The old chair would rock backwards and forwards and side to side as we screamed with delight, clinging to his neck so that we would not be flung into the raging billows all around us.

My parents were members of the Pentecostal Assemblies of God Church in Preston and among the first to be baptised in the Holy Spirit when the "Fire fell" during the Sunderland Revival at the beginning of the 20th Century.

My memory of those Sundays, however, is the long distances we had to walk to the church, and how tired we were at the end of the day. My father would not hear of us boarding a tram, so eventually we were sent to a little mission nearer home. It was there at the age of five that I made the greatest decision of my life — to follow Jesus.

Child conversions, if not actually frowned upon, were not encouraged in those days. My conversion was on a Sunday evening in November 1918, kneeling by the wooden form with a dear old saint of God, Mr Dalby. The great transaction was done and for me the beginning of a wonderful, thrilling, adventurous life.

At the age of twelve years I followed the Lord through the "Waters of Baptism" and also received the "Baptism of the Spirit"; my own personal Pentecost.

These were wonderful, stirring experiences. I suppose in one sense of the word I had not known sin. In our sheltered home life, even slang was discouraged, so that I was never aware of any great change after "conversion" and was often tormented with doubts and fears as to the reality of my Salvation until that wonderful evening, in the upper room of the Assembly, when I was gloriously baptised in the Holy Spirit.

Since then I have known a deep, settled peace which has remained throughout my life. Also at the age of 12 God called me to be a missionary. I shall never forget the moment when "He spoke", when the consciousness of the call of God dawned on my soul. The blessed sacredness and solemnity of that hour when I heard God's voice, somehow awakened in me, child though I was, a sense of urgency and responsibility.

I recall how I trembled on the verge of this new vision; how it engulfed and separated me from the chatter of my friends who shared the same gallery steps in that crowded missionary meeting on Easter

Monday afternoon. A fierce struggle went on in my heart and as a real home girl and not a ready adventurer I feared the thought of leaving home, parents, friends, and security, to put the sea between myself and all I held dear. Though I trembled, the Mighty Conqueror of Hearts won, and I was able to say yes to Him who had in a new way, become my Lord and Master.

From then on my life was geared to one end: to fulfil the call of God. Of course there were setbacks, disappointments, heartaches and times when doubts and failures obscured the vision.

I was tempted by offers of marriage and a career, but the insistent call of God could not be denied.

2

Nursing Days

In May 1934 I left home to begin Nurse Training in Birmingham. Launched out into the world, I knew the thrilling experience of the God-directed life.

As I stood on that bleak station platform waiting for the train, with a lump in my throat, God was already providing for my first venture into the unknown. Gathered to wish me "God speed" were quite a large number of friends from the Assembly. I remember it was on this occasion, perhaps more than in later years when I sailed for China, that the tears were shed and the tender little hymns were sung.

I was the first young person from the Church to be venturing forth into the wide world, and as that great powerful engine snorted its way into the station, I was lovingly commended to God's care and protection.

Mother had already carried my case into one of the carriages, assuring me that I would have a travelling companion in my compartment, a young lady. Imagine my joy and amazement to learn that she too was on her way to begin Nurse Training in the same hospital! How gracious is our God, how marvellous is His kindness towards us. The grief of that parting was in no small measure assuaged by the reminder of His going before.

I must spare a word of commendation for my mother. She was a great woman of God. She too, in her early teens had heard the call for missionary service but, as the eldest of a large family, was never able to fulfil that call. When she later married, each child was lovingly given back to God. In turn I was taken up to the assembly and in a simple act of dedication given back to Him, with this difference: so complete was that act, Mother never again laid claim to me.

I was leaving home now, at a very critical time in our home affairs when I knew it was at great sacrifice.

Some years later, in fact only twelve months before I sailed for China, Mother was to be suddenly widowed. Despite the drastic change this would bring about in her circumstances, and although I was prepared to stay and care for her, she insisted on my going, emphatic in her belief that God would supply all her need.

Enough to say that she lacked nothing; that her latter days were better than her former, blessed with the "Blessings that make rich".

In the meantime, Birmingham, that great city of the Midlands, had been troubled with white slave traffic and New Street Station, where we pulled in, was the hotbed for these illicit proceedings. Young girls were met and whisked off, never to be seen again.

We were relieved therefore to be met by a nurse friend of my travelling companion, who escorted us to the hospital and initiated us into the mysteries of our strange new world.

Here even the making up of uniform was a major operation with its dress, apron, stiff collar, cuffs and belt and not the least, the cap; a regulation uniform that made me feel an entirely new kind of being.

To this day, I can never forget the desolate, lonely feeling that swept over me when I awakened next morning to the clanging of a bell and a strange impersonal voice, shouting, "6 o'clock, Nurses!"

Dudley Road Hospital was one of the largest in the city, averaging 1,000 beds, with nursing staff of probably around 350. Imagine us, struggling as quickly as possible into our strange new apparel and finding, on presenting ourselves in the dining room, hundreds of nurses in immaculate starched caps and aprons, with polished shoes. Girls of all ages, sizes, shapes and colour, who fell upon the food without so much as a glance at the obviously new recruits. We must have looked, and certainly felt, objects of misery, as we stood uncertainly in the doorway. In seconds, we found ourselves at one of the tables, lost in the uniformity of dress and chatter, and too alone and miserable to eat the bacon and toast without almost choking.

Outside the dining room I was grabbed by one nurse, my friend by another and we were hauled off to our respective wards.

Before leaving my cubicle that morning I had

commended myself to God, praying for strength and courage to live for Him in my new surroundings. I knew the necessity of nailing my colours to the mast and prayed that my faith might not fail in the hour of temptation.

Happily I didn't know how soon it was to be tested. My heart had already almost failed me when I saw so many efficient-looking nurses, scurrying off to their different wards. The similarity in dress did nothing to make me feel one of them. We reached the ward at last and joined a happy group in the kitchen.

I was shown the ropes by the senior nurse and as we were about to go into the ward, she mentioned a strange and unusual letter she had received the day before from some unknown lady. She said it was hilarious and well worth reading before starting work. In the bathroom she read us an amazing letter.

The writer, a Christian lady, evidently deeply concerned for the soul of this particular girl, had made plain the Gospel of salvation, quoting much of the 53rd Chapter of Isaiah, and appealing to her to get right with God. Listening to the Scriptures she quoted, I heard the glowing testimony of salvation.

Noting the burden that throbbed in every word and the impassioned appeal at the end, my heart was thrilled just to belong to the same wonderful Lord and to be able to identify myself with the writer.

There was only one thing left now for me to do and that was what I did. I made a full confession of my faith. Scared though I was I was quick to perceive that God in His wonderful thoughtfulness had engineered this occasion so that I, His weak erring child, should have an opportunity of doing what I had prayed for grace to do.

Later in the day, during visiting hours I was given the opportunity to witness to the staff about salvation and what Jesus meant to me.

It wasn't long before the whole hospital knew whose I was and whom I served, so that from then on I was never troubled to buy raffle tickets, or invited to hospital shows or dances. Christian nurses and sisters sought me out, welcomed me to their little devotional meetings and gave me opportunities to serve. If we confess Him before men and women, He will confess us before His Father in Heaven.

In retrospect, those early months of training hold many painful memories of adjustment and learning. I draw the veil over some of the outrageous mistakes I made, when answering the phone and getting the right message seemed a major accomplishment. Would I ever understand the Birmingham dialect?

I also want to gloss over the humiliating experience of mistaking the newspaperman for the doctor; the trips across to the Pathological Laboratory every morning with a tray of urine specimens — paper cups in situ — in a capricious wind ... when even the elements seemed against me! And the horror of remembering cuffs left behind on the ward as Matron approached.

All these bitter-sweet memories, some frightening, some uplifting, some with laughter, some with tears, some with sadness and some with happiness, all made up the whole of those early nursing days.

One of the happiest chores of the day was that of accompanying a discharged patient, with relatives, to the exit door of the hospital. But even this had its moments. The intricacies of operating the lift with its rows of buttons and no indications as to which floor, made all attempts to appear in charge futile, as a few joyrides finally resulted in my conducting the — by then hysterical — little group to the ground floor.

The first three months I was dreadfully homesick, and the longing for home was almost unbearable. Sometimes I wandered around that vast city, lonely and heartsick, yet God gave me so many tokens of His care and thoughtfulness: unexpected Christian acquaintances; the kindness of apparent strangers; the friendly policeman; and most of all, His companionship.

Looking back now, from the safety of years of confident trust and many proofs of His unfailing goodness, my heart is thrilled again. What a glorious thing it is to be out on God!

Many and varied were the experiences during the wonderful happy years which followed. I remember taking a journey from Manchester to London during the war years to attend an interview for a Sister's post at East Ham Memorial Hospital. An air raid on London had delayed our train — leaving little time for me to reach my destination at the appointed time. Apprehension almost spoiled the excitement of my first visit to the metropolis.

The milling rush-hour crowds, the awful confusion of the underground, made me hopelessly muddled and lost, until I remembered to lift my heart to Him who is ever mindful of His own, who tenderly watches over us, every step, every mile of the way.

Glancing around, I saw a porter and when I asked

the way, he pointed to a lady wearing a red hat who, he explained, was going in my direction. Imagine my surprise to discover she was also a Hospital Sister, bound for the same interview! A coincidence? Perhaps, but to the child of God on the way, a very precious coincidence. And life was full of these.

"The steps of a good man are ordered by the Lord and He delights in his way."

There were difficult experiences, of course, when there seemed no rhyme or reason to what was happening, when there seemed no answer to prayer, just blind trust in the One who never errs.

At the end of my first three months of initial training I was told I was not strong enough in health to carry on with my nursing career.

How could this be?

I needed this career to become a missionary, to fulfil God's call. Could I be mistaken in the call? No! Never! I was absolutely sure that God had called me. This was a real test of my assurance of hearing God's voice.

Christian friends and family prayed and supported me through this time until God opened a door in a smaller hospital where I was able to complete my general and midwifery training. In Hallam Hospital, West Bromwich, I seemed to be the only Christian nurse. How impatiently I awaited the arrival of each new school of nurse students, eagerly looking out for signs of girls with the Christian faith. I was hungry for fellowship with my own kind.

Those bright spots in the week when, with an odd evening off duty, I could get to the services at the little

Elim church in the town, were like an oasis in the desert.

God graciously heard my prayer for Christian companionship and before the end of the first year there were four Pentecostal nurses.

"Foursquare Gospellers" they nicknamed us. We didn't mind that, providing we had each other. We shared our joys, sorrows, trials, and difficulties, and enjoyed marvellous fellowship in the evenings after arduous days, when we talked, comforted, helped and prayed for one another.

Training days were not all joy and sunshine, however; work was hard and heavy and the day long. Even off duty was taken up by attending lectures. There was the sharp-tongued Sister and the worried Staff Nurse to harass us. When we eventually came off duty, it was with tired, aching bodies and burning feet.

Our narrow beds with their horse hair mattresses were well appreciated as we just lay and relaxed and talked over events of the day.

We doctored our feet regularly with methylated spirits and powder and somehow managed to go back on duty the next morning, looking sprightly and energetic as ever.

There came a time of bitter persecution, when Matron summoned me repeatedly to her office and lectured me on my so-called religious beliefs "amounting to mania," she said. I was instructed to stop the prayer meeting in my room.

Off duty was then arranged in such a way as to prevent the four of us from having time off together. Privileges were cut and in many ways we were humiliated and even bullied, until one day when, having summoned me again to her office, Matron looked searchingly, almost appealingly into my face and said, "Nurse Bowkett, what exactly do you believe?"

So I was given the opportunity to testify to her all about my early conversion, baptism in water and the Holy Spirit, how God had healed, guided and made life so wonderful, meaning so much more than earthly position and material prosperity.

Matron listened, with her head in her hands, interrupting now and again with a question, but listening on the whole to what I had to say. Shortly after this incident she retired, and I have not seen her again. The Word says in Eccl 11:1 to *"Cast your bread upon the waters, for after many days you will find it again."*

Training days over and the coveted S.R.N., S.C.M. after my name, I turned my eyes to the whitened harvest fields of the Far East. But war clouds were already gathering in Britain and before any definite steps could be taken, we were plunged into the holocaust of war, with all its subsequent misery.

3

Wartime in Manchester

There followed six years of hardship, deprivation and misery, with wearisome days and terror-filled nights. Every day brought bad news; partings, and tragedies beyond description. Our lives consisted of queues, bombings, waitings, and longings.

Even so, we had happy times, hilarious moments; sleeping in the shelters and escapades under cover of the blackout. Morale was high and we learned to live with the noise of bombs and the uncertainties of life, snatching at brief intervals of lull.

In Manchester where, as a Staff Midwife I was in a reserved occupation for the duration of the war, there were nights of continuous bombing. Each evening saw us, clad in Siren Suits, pillows under our arm, wending our way to the communal air raid shelter at the end of the street.

The nights were long and we wearied of these all too frequent jaunts across the road, so it was a tremendous relief when the cellar of our own nurses' home was reinforced for use during the raids. We spent more and more time in the confines of that particular cellar as the nightly raids increased, until it culminated in one terrifying night of blitz, when Manchester was bombed from end to end.

It was Christmas 1941. When the sirens sounded at 6 p.m. Christmas Eve, we little thought what the night would bring, the horror and destruction, the imminence of death that was to be our lot before the morning.

Was it a sixth sense that made Matron leave just a token force on duty, sending the rest of us to the basement shelters? The patients also, except those in need of labour ward facilities and staff, were transferred to the reinforced cellars.

Before 10 p.m. the city was ablaze with incendiary bombs. A full moon sailed majestically overhead and with its light and the many fires raging, it was possible to read comfortably the small print of a newspaper.

Manchester was a sitting duck for the enemy. All through the long hours of that night, we huddled together in the basement cellar, hours of such anguish and fear as are utterly indescribable. The roar and crash of falling masonry, the breaking of glass and the incessant drone of the bombers overhead, drowned at times the shouts and screams of the injured and dying.

Tensed and white faced, we awaited our turn, watching the walls of our shelter tremble and sag with the blast of each bomb, but amazingly they righted themselves and remained intact all through that terrifying night.

Bombs hurtled down with a regularity that was frightening, miraculously missing the house where we nurses lived, but demolishing four-storey buildings just a hundred yards up the road. We twelve or more nurses and a Senior Home Sister felt very much alone and at the mercy of these fiendish bombers. No one came near except one lone medical student who picked his way over the debris around about 2:00 a.m. to see if we were still alive, cheering us no end by informing us that the rest of the building was in ruins and that he had experienced the utmost difficulty in finding us!

We begged him to stay, but he told us there was utter chaos across at the hospital; the Manchester Royal Infirmary next door to us had suffered a direct hit and the students' hostel, just across the road, was practically in ruins.

It seemed the night would never end. The bombing continued mercilessly from 6:00 o'clock in the evening, until 6:00 o'clock the next morning.

Our pet dog went mad with the awful din and noise and raced off outside, never to be seen again. It took all the will-power we possessed, to remain in that confined place, when all hell was let loose around us. There was an insane urge to get outside and run away from it all. Even so, I want to testify that I never really felt alone. Someone stood by me, all through the long dark night, into whose safe keeping I had committed my life many years ago. I was most surely aware of His protecting presence, so that amid it all, I knew a wonderful abiding peace.

More than once during the night, I was asked to pray for our safety, and found it easy to talk of His wonderful saving grace.

The sound of the All Clear at 6:00 a.m. was the most wonderful sound we had ever heard. To find us all sound in life and limb was nothing short of a miracle.

We had miraculously survived.

The devastation was heartbreaking to see. Huge piles of debris, all that remained of the lovely gracious buildings of yester year. A few remaining shells of houses stood with windows blown out, doors blasted off their hinges and shreds of curtain fluttering in the morning breeze as the dust and smoke settled.

A dozen or more army officers had been billeted just up the road. As we stood in the devastation we became aware that we could hear faint cries for help above the stillness of life and death. Later, we were to see those officers being dug out by the rescue squad, many of them already dead.

We ourselves were homeless, our belongings buried beneath the rubble. We were still in uniform, but so begrimed by the dust and dirt, they never really became clean again and it was a long time before the grime was really washed away from the skin or that we felt tingling fresh again. For the next few months we lived in a temporary dwelling place in Victoria Park, about a mile from the hospital. The conditions were grim, offset only by the novelty of the situation.

We all slept in one room; two rows of seven beds packed tightly together. To get to one's bed was a work of art, to leave it once having settled was not tolerated. There was room only for one chair to accommodate all our clothes, so that the last one in bed had of necessity to be the first one up the next morning, making it easier in the darkness to pick up the right uniform and underwear.

There was no blackout at the windows and we were only allowed one very dim light, so it isn't difficult to imagine the utter chaos which prevailed every morning as we sought to get ready and out of the house in time for the longish walk to the hospital, where we were on duty at 7:30 a.m. This didn't always work out. Garments, hastily shed the night before, were sometimes hopelessly mixed up. Frayed tempers and a strained atmosphere prevailed at times.

The very early mornings were not conducive to hilarity, though we usually managed to see the funny side of it all by the evening, with the result that long after we should have been asleep, smothered laughter and whisperings made this also difficult.

I resist the temptation to write of all six war years, when the raids continued and we hardly ever knew the joy of a complete night's sleep. When queues were longer and ration books and coupons added to the difficulties of shopping. When we put up with the boring diet of dried milk, dried eggs and even dried bananas.

Travelling too became increasingly difficult and wearisome in the extreme, mile-long queues for buses and trains which were dimly lit and badly heated even on the coldest days.

In spite of the frustrations, however, there was an atmosphere of cheerfulness and hope. The amazing courage and resilience of individuals was wonderful

19

to see, as the threads of daily life were picked up after being torn apart.

There were the amusing incidents also, too numerous to recount, though one of them readily comes to mind of a little old lady, who in a queue one day, after waiting some considerable time asked "What are we queuing for?"

"The Tales of Hoffman," was the reply.

"Oh well," she said, "I might as well wait, I suppose they will do as well as anything for lunch."

It was a time of laughter and tears, and after a while, peace. The church bells rang, children laughed and played, good humour bubbled over. Bunting and flags appeared as if by magic and street parties were the order of the day.

V.E. Day (Victory in Europe) was a day of jubilation, of gaiety and I regret to say, of drink, with resulting cascades of laughter and hangovers, the aftermath of which was the realisation that peace too must be won.

So many were homeless, sick and wounded in spirit and there was a real need for comfort and aid of so many kinds.

Most of all the need was for Jesus.

4

Preparation

As life resumed normality, my thoughts turned once more to God's call. For six years, all missionary activity had been at a standstill; six wasted years, or was it? Now that I was 32 years of age, it would almost appear so, except that God's timing is perfect.

The last boat to China in 1940 had carried with it my fiancé, but in the ensuing years, with the irregularities of the postal system, the seeming hopelessness of ever sailing myself, and due to war activities, including the evacuation of all missionaries from China, we had broken off our engagement. This led to a period of such spiritual darkness for me, that I wondered if I had mistaken my call.

God's ways are not our ways, however, nor His thoughts, our thoughts.

I had already been accepted as a Missionary Candidate, but now due to my broken engagement, my application was to be reconsidered by the Missionary Council. In the dark days that followed, God graciously showed me His power in a mighty move of Salvation at Crumpsall Hospital, where I was now Labour Ward Sister. He also proved to me that His call is not circumscribed or bound by Missionary Boards or government.

It leaps all these obstacles and is fulfilled in God.

About this time, I was asked to take over the Nurses Christian Movement group in the hospital. This I did, and found a very nice company gathered at the first meeting, most of whom were good religious women.

Christ, however, never wanted us to be "religious", He wants us to be Christ followers, fully involved and committed to Him, so here was a challenge.

I was junior to most of those who gathered and knew any interference with their set religious ways would not be appreciated; but God takes the weak things of this world to confound the mighty.

One evening after speaking on that great woman of the Bible, Ruth, I noticed a student nurse moved to tears. She disappeared immediately after the Service but the following day handed me a letter in which she expressed her need and desire for the Salvation of which I had spoken the previous evening.

This marked the beginning of a wonderful move of God and many nurses turned to our Lord and Saviour, Jesus Christ. The entire hospital was affected in some way or another as each week the power of God was displayed in changed, regenerated lives. Their radiant faces resulted in us being nicknamed "The Lights" and a table was set aside in the dining room for our exclusive use, known to all as the "Lights table."

The desire for God's Word led us to start Bible Studies in my room and, using a model of the Tabernacle, we spent many happy hours studying the types and truths of what was the forerunner of the Temple and what it symbolised. We spent many glorious times of prayer together.

There were days of fellowship and relaxation in the country; exciting times when we visited the churches, testifying in word and song. Twice we visited my home Assembly in Preston, where several of our number were baptised by immersion.

These were wonderful, wonderful days.

About this time Elsie Norcliffe, a Staff Nurse, joined us and helped greatly in our outreach. Her beautiful singing voice never failed to bless and her many talents were used in the service of the Lord.

Sister Keay, an evangelical Church of England girl, also joined us and together we shared the joys, responsibilities and burden of this growing work.

Sometime later I moved to Whisten Hospital near Liverpool as Midwifery Night Supervisor and again had the joy of seeing God move in the same way. Elsie Norcliffe had, quite unknown to me, applied to the same hospital for a post as Staff Midwife — so amazingly we were together again and ready for what God would do there.

There was no Nurses Christian Movement, but we

quickly started one and just as quickly saw God working with us, patients, nurses, doctors, maids, and porters, all came under the conviction of the Holy Spirit and were wonderfully saved.

One exceptional incident occurred at this time. A little girl, Claire, who was four years old, was admitted to the Children's Ward in a moribund condition, that is: with little sign of life. This child lay for six to seven weeks sustained by naso-gastric feeding and specialised nursing care. She was nicknamed "Sleeping Beauty" and was the concern of the entire hospital. Consultants and doctors, specialists in every field, sought for a cause; but finding none, could give no reliable treatment either.

The male Staff Nurse in charge of the Ward at the time loved and honoured the Lord Jesus, witnessing to a young Jewish Houseman who became interested in Salvation. He was intrigued to know that as a band of Christians we were praying for Claire's healing.

One never to be forgotten day, while Staff Nurse and the doctor were standing talking at the foot of the bed, Claire suddenly opened her eyes and started to sing that lovely children's chorus, "All the way to Calvary, He went for me." The doctor was so moved that he recorded this on Claire's medical notes, "This child for the first time this morning, sang these words, 'All the way to Calvary He went for me'. "

Claire's subsequent recovery was the topic of conversation in and around the hospital for many months to come. On the day of her discharge, the nurse carried Claire to the window and asked, "What are the birds singing?"

"Jesus loves me," was the reply of this little miracle

of God's grace.

How easy it was at that time to talk to people about Him.

As a group of Christian nurses, we were invited to take the services in many of the local churches. We enjoyed fellowship with the Holiness Churches and various Salvation Army Corps around the area.

Another great baptismal service was held in Preston Assembly, when we hired a 45-seater coach and private cars to convey those who wanted to follow the Lord through the waters of baptism.

What compensation all this was for the distress and disappointment of a broken engagement. I remember one lady remarking, "You may not have natural children, but God has certainly given you spiritual ones."

God's moment is worth waiting for
Though precious years may flee,
In silence He is perfecting
That which concerneth thee.

These words were quoted to me by a friend, when one day I was chafing at the delay in fulfilling my life's ambition; how true they proved to be. When the perfecting processes of the Master Potter are completed, then He will put the vessel to use.

So through joys, sorrows, trials, difficulties, successes and failures, He gently prepared me for the day when I received a letter to attend an interview with the Assemblies of God Missionary Council.

It was with some trepidation as to the outcome

Ruth as a nursing Sister

that I journeyed to London, but God had appointed the time. So I was accepted as their missionary candidate and told to prepare for an early sailing. As I continued my work with this in mind, so wonderfully happy in His will, an unexpected and tremendous sorrow befell our family.

My father became ill and died within five weeks.

This bereavement was the first major sorrow in our close-knit family circle and was a grievous trial. We were completely shaken by it. But Mother again was an inspiration to us all, calm and dignified in her sorrow she proved the Lord's unfailing strength and so infused into each one of us some of her tremendous courage and fortitude.

How would this change of circumstances affect my future missionary career? As the eldest daughter I felt it was my duty to stay at home and support Mother.

She was adamant, however, in her refusal to accept this, confident that God would fulfil His promise to be *"a husband to the widow."*

The following month therefore, I resigned from hospital service and began itinerary work around the Assemblies.

Never before had I been so overwhelmingly conscious of my weaknesses and inadequacies as when I stood before some of those congregations with the responsibility of delivering the word of God and presenting it in such a way that people could receive it and be blessed by it.

I was continually conscious of my need of the refreshing and invigorating unction of the Holy Spirit and was repeatedly driven to my knees to seek that help. In utter weakness I would stand to minister and then witness the mighty demonstration of the power of God as He, the Holy Spirit, took over with satisfying results.

It was at this time that He gave me wonderful tokens of His love and care. My outstanding needs were met and lovely friendships formed that were to prove a blessing right through all the years of missionary service and to this present day.

These friends became faithful prayer partners.

5

The Great Unknown

The fateful telegram arrived unexpectedly one Thursday evening in early September 1946. Mother and I returned from a Bible study meeting to find it lying on the floor behind the door. My heart gave a lurch as with trembling fingers I opened the envelope and read: "Berth booked on Otranto sailing Hong Kong September 14th. Wire acceptance."

Shock, dismay, and joy, mingled with fear for Mother registered on my face. How would the inevitable parting affect her? Since my father's death almost ten months previously we had spent as much time as possible together in my endeavour to fill the gap. Now in a confusion of thoughts I looked at her white strained face with misgivings.

Then God spoke to my failing heart with a clear word of direction, "Matt 10:37: *'If you love your father or mother more than you love me, you are not worthy of being mine'."* (TLB)   Peace flooded my whole being as the decision was made; Mother's future too was in His hands.

The next day a letter of confirmation also informed me that I would be sailing with Mr and Mrs R. Colley, their three children, and Miss Hewitt. This was cheering news and I began to look forward tremendously to our going.

Two weeks of pandemonium followed, with carpets rolled up in one of the bedrooms to accommodate cable cases and boxes of all kinds. Friends from the Assembly assisted with sewing, sorting and packing; one brother stencilled, another corded boxes, while a third, an excise officer, passed each package, sealing them with his own seal. Only later, when passing through the Customs, did I fully appreciate this valuable contribution.

How true are Samuel Chadwick's words, "There are no people like God's people".

Meanwhile the day of separation drew near.

It had been my joy many times while working near Liverpool, to spend days off with an ex-colleague and friend, Sister Keay. Our meeting place however, I had detested. It was the wharf. Many times I had looked at the cold grey waters and thought of the parting to come. But as Mother and I breakfasted together on that memorable morning of September 1946, there was a serenity about her that was a rebuke to all tears, as with such confidence she read Isaiah 55, making verse 12 my particular portion for the day. *"So you will go out with joy and be led out in peace."*

As we travelled to London and then on to Southampton, questions arose in my mind. Would I measure up to the standards of a good missionary? Would the learning of a new language prove too difficult? What could I do to ensure Mother's well-being and financial security? When I return in 5 to 6 years' time will home, family and friends be just as I left them?

These thoughts were difficult and stressful; but I found peace by spending time in the presence of the Lord and through His wonderful Word. Psalm 91:2 was a particular help to me at this time *"My God. In Him will I trust"*.

At the quayside, the bustle and excitement of formalities allowed time for only a quick embrace then, after placing hand luggage in our cabins, we returned on deck to scan the group waiting on the wharf.

A shout and a wave, the clanging of the ship's bell, the casting of the moorings and slowly and majestically the great vessel sailed out to sea.

I was so glad just then of the company of travelling companions as I watched that tiny figure, my mother, waving both arms until distance dimmed the view. The memory will remain with me always. There have been many painful goodbyes since then, but the deep sense of sacrifice contained in that parting bound Mother and me in some degree with the mystical fellowship of Christ's sufferings.

Within a few years Mother had waved goodbye to her two sons also; my eldest brother emigrating to the United States, and the youngest to New Zealand. Returning home after the third quayside parting, the feeling of bereavement and desolation was almost too much for my brave mother.

Graciously God met her as she turned to the "Cheering Words" calendar for the text of the day, and read: 1 Sam 1:8: *"you have me—isn't that better than having ten sons?"* Comfort and strength flowed into her again.

The Otranto was a one class boat; a converted troop ship now on her first post-war voyage to China. Conditions therefore were still rather grim. The cabins were large with twenty-eight or more bunks in tiers, utilising all available space. Six washbasins lined up along one wall were for everyone's use. At the end of each bunk was a large nail which answered for a wardrobe (and chest of drawers). One or two chairs completed the furniture.

There was a large missionary contingent on board and Miss Hewitt and I shared a cabin with 23 other passengers of like minds.

Nevertheless, I must confess there was a bit of complaining as we tried to unpack. Inevitable I suppose under the circumstances, when one's entire wardrobe for the voyage of a month's duration had to hang on a single nail.

I remember there was only room in each gangway for one cabin trunk to be opened at a time so the rest of us sat on our bunks until it came to our turn. Very soon the cabin resembled a jumble sale.

It was hard enough staying sanctified when the going was smooth, but on the second day in the notorious Bay of Biscay many of us were confined to the cabin and the six washbasins proved quite inadequate in the throes of seasickness.

In spite of the cramped conditions and the discomfort of sleeping quarters I must admit that I found the whole voyage gloriously exciting, and we had plenty of fun and fellowship. There was always something new to see, a school of whales, flying fish and the amusing gambolling of the dolphins.

Then there was the never to be forgotten sail through the Suez Canal, so narrow in places that our great liner seemed to touch the shore.

What a sight to see the Arabs as they rode by on their camels and the encampments of those nomadic travellers, then surprisingly an Englishman's compound with its green lawns, trees and flowering shrubs; a cool inviting vista amidst the barrenness of a sun-baked world. The evergreen appearance, we learned, was the result of perpetual watering.

We had interesting visits ashore in the various ports where the ship docked, and in Singapore I had my first introduction to Chinese life in real style. While we were sweltering in the terrible heat, three days in dock, no refreshing breezes blowing through the portholes and almost overcome by it all, an invitation to go ashore and spend a whole day with a Christian gentleman in his palatial home, was a blessing indeed.

This lovely gesture included all the missionaries — ninety-two in all — who enjoyed the freedom of the extensive grounds which included a swimming pool. Truly a place of refreshing.

Life on board became very organised in a comparatively short time. School began for the children and the missionaries held a Bible study each morning, with devotional sessions throughout the day.

Occasionally in the late evening I would stand at

the prow of the ship, under a magnificent starlit sky, watching the great liner steer a straight course through the trackless deep, carrying me ever nearer to the unknown.

Our last day in the China Sea was very exciting indeed. Coming in to land on the tail of a typhoon was just what was needed to wean us from life aboard. Practically every passenger was seasick and therefore confined to his or her cabin.

The marvellous landfall dinner which we had looked forward to so much proved to be a fiasco and the sight of land was an anticipated haven for us all.

As we sailed into calmer waters we noticed lots of smaller craft, launches, speedboats, sailing boats and even sampans coming out to meet and escort us into the harbour, manned, we learned later, by husbands and sweethearts of some of our fellow passengers. After six or seven years of war, spent by many of them in Japanese concentration camps in Hong Kong, they were now to be reunited; the emotions were overpowering.

Some of the women had to be restrained from jumping into the smaller vessels as they recognised their beloved menfolk.

We were thrilled as we sailed slowly into the beautiful harbour to hear the strains of some of our old English and Scottish songs. Imagine a Gurkha regiment in full Scottish regalia playing on bagpipes, "My Bonnie lies over the ocean".

What a colourful scene: vivid blue sky, white, red and gold sails dotted over the sparkling water and the quayside thronged with eager excited people. Chinese coolies jostled with the Colonials in their smart drill and tropical suits, and the ladies wore their brightly coloured costumes and pretty dresses. Dominating the entire scene as it towered into the sky, was that well-known landmark, 'The Peak' serving as a magnificent backcloth to the colourful scene of the harbour.

No sooner was the gangway lowered than there was a terrific rush as the menfolk tried to get to their wives and sweethearts. Such kissing and cuddling there never was. I felt a lump in my throat and a prickling in the back of my eyes as I looked on. At that moment I couldn't imagine anything worse than to arrive on foreign soil and have no one to greet me on the quayside. To gaze down from the deck of the ship on to the sea of upturned faces and not recognise one of them, must be the acme of loneliness.

Before I could indulge in any more self-pity, however, we heard a hearty "Praise the Lord!", and it was our turn to be embraced and welcomed. Mr and Mrs Rousseau, Pentecostal missionaries, friends of Miss Hewitt, who were stationed in Kowloon just across the water, took us into their care, and the awful lost feeling vanished.

How kind they were, helping us with all the formalities, the supervising of that great pile of luggage, which had to be left in a "go-down" for the night, then taking us to their lovely home where we were made so comfortable. So many years ago and yet it seems like yesterday. One does not easily forget such friends. They were so lavish in their kindness towards us and so helpful, that the necessary business was negotiated without a hitch.

I will never forget either my first night on Chinese soil, or the speedy acquaintance with some of the night life of the city.

Following an early supper the three Colley children went to bed. They were tired and over-excited so, as an inducement to sleep I went to tell them a bedtime story. Their three Safari beds were low on the floor but with mosquito nets in place they were safe from intruders.

I was still only halfway through my story when I saw the biggest, most fearsome spider crawl up the wall right near the children's heads. Having heard about the famous tarantula, my eyes were transfixed with horror and it took all the will-power I possessed not to scream. The encroaching darkness fortunately helped to mask my natural revulsion and fear and so prevented the possibility of hysteria. Thankfully, the children never knew and the spider disappeared.

Later on, trying to get to sleep ourselves, we were awakened by a dreadful row between two Chinese women in the street below. One has to see a fight of this nature to appreciate its utter depravity. Fighting cats pale into insignificance; screams and shouts rent the air, increasing in ferocity and it was with these sounds still ringing in our ears that we eventually fell asleep.

Sometime in the early hours I awakened to different noises altogether, scratchings, scufflings, and squeakings. The room seemed full of sound. Was every night to be like this? I lay trembling, fearing almost to breathe, so thankful for the protection of the mosquito net which kept all kinds of intruders at bay.

The next morning all was quiet; but around my elbow, which had evidently been up against the net,

Miss Hewitt counted no less than 120 mosquito bites! Lured by the rare treat of a drop of fresh English blood they had taken their fill.

We quickly identified the other sounds of the night too. My large leather handbag, specially provided for the safe keeping of my passport and other documents, had been attacked by rats, a large hole eaten in the side. Some of my papers were bitten into and the Hong Kong dollars, obtained only the previous evening, almost entirely devoured.

6

China at Last

Hong Kong was a fascinating place. We enjoyed every minute of our stay there, walking down the streets, seeing the rich human life going on all around, the laughter, the good-natured buying and selling and the contentment of the people in spite of evident poverty.

I shall never forget the precarious ride on the bus, when the vehicle was so overloaded, the people were hanging on like grim death and still they allowed us to board. It was little short of a miracle that we reached our destination safely.

Browsing around the shops was fascinating; rarely have I seen such a display of goods. The gorgeous silks, the most beautiful hand-embroidered clothes, and novelties of every description.

Exquisitely carved tables and cedar chests, precious stones, jewellery, ivory and brass-work, charming little porcelain figures, the finest of bamboo scrolls, all made us wish for more of that necessary substance which missionaries seem to be constantly without.

The clever workmanship of their lovely cane chairs, baskets, tables, fans and even cradles, had us counting our pennies to see if funds might extend to one small piece.

One glorious day we spent on the Peak, travelling by the funicular railway to the top. What a wonderful view from that vantage point, over the harbour and well out to sea. Strange that it should be that very day when the Otranto loosed her moorings and set sail again for England. We could see it quite plainly from the top of the Peak and there were a few pangs of homesickness at that moment. Resolutely we turned away; for ahead was an entirely new life of glorious opportunity for service, of proving God and seeing His outworking.

In the meantime, Mr Colley had been making preparations for the last lap of our journey to Kunming, the capital of Yunnan Province, South West China. There was one main route by air and we womenfolk with the children would be taking our flight as soon as possible; but Mr Colley was planning to travel overland with our boxes. We had several tons of luggage between us and this created a real problem.

All mail and road services were disorganised — the result of long years of war. Roads were dangerous, beset by bandits and robbers, so it was with some degree of apprehension that we eventually saw the two men off on their long, hazardous journey, Mr Colley being accompanied by a Baptist missionary friend.

Two days later the rest of us left Hong Kong for Canton, where there seemed to be more possibility of booking an early flight to Kunming. We were to stay with Mr and Mrs Kholls of the German Lutheran Mission, on the far bank of the River Pearl.

It was good to see someone waiting for us at the railway terminus to assist with luggage and to guide us safely through the masses of people and the equally bewildering maze of streets, until we came to the waterside, where we quickly booked a large sampan to take us over to the other shore.

All the Lutheran missionaries were gathered for a Conference at that time and consequently every available room was taken. But to accommodate us, Mrs Kholls housed our party in the organ loft of the church in the compound. What a strange situation that was: no curtains or niceties, just six camp beds, bare boards, and a wash hand basin and jug. Once again we were tormented all night by rats, but it was surprising how quickly we adapted ourselves and were able to sleep through the noise, the novelty of it all lending an air of romance, especially for the children, who thought of it as one great adventure.

Mr Colley had called into Canton en route and had managed to book a flight for Mrs Colley and the children. Unfortunately Miss Hewitt and I were delayed a whole month as seats booked on the plane were lost time and again through the bribery of influential Chinese.

Canton was a large, thriving, bustling city, considerably overpopulated; the streets thronged with people: the rich, the poor, the educated, the ignorant, the thrifty and the careless. Shoulder to shoulder we rubbed up against them; degrading sights too. Emaciated beggars left to die on the streets, (the passers-by showing no pity or compassion).

We saw strange foodstuffs on sale too. One day among the display of fruits and vegetables in the market, their shiny backs glistening in the sun, was a dish of roasted cockroaches; quite revolting to me but considered a delicacy in China.

The friendly attitude of the Hong Kong people was sadly lacking here. There was instead, a marked anti-foreign feeling. They looked on us with suspicion, so that when requiring a rickshaw we had to spend time bargaining for the price and usually there were angry words before they would agree to take us. We also heard many disturbing accounts of the rough treatment some of the foreigners had received. One notable trick was to snatch a lady's hat while she was riding in a rickshaw, and then grab her handbag as she endeavoured to rescue her hat.

An unfortunate incident happened one day when Miss Hewitt and I were strolling through the lanes at the back of the compound. I innocently plucked from the hedgerow one of their sacred flowers. Immediately there was a tirade from a group of workers in the paddy fields nearby and in spite of Miss Hewitt's attempt at an explanation, they chased us, throwing huge stones at us as they ran.

Later, in the safety of my room and shaken by what had happened, I had certain misgivings as to whether I could love these people enough to spend the rest of my life working with them. Miss Hewitt, realising my state of mind, prayed with me that God would give me His compassion. Thank God He did — so that to this day my love for the Chinese is deep and lasting.

I suppose if I had not been eagerly studying the Chinese language I might have acquired a considerable knowledge of German during our stay in Canton. There were eighteen to twenty missionaries gathered together there and every mealtime Miss Hewitt and I were obliged to listen to German being spoken. It was Mrs Kholls' policy to change our places at every meal so we could get to know one another. This was a commendable idea I thought, providing we understood the German language; but we scarcely knew a couple of words and felt very miserable at times, separated as we were by the length of the dining table.

There were two very nice single ladies, however, who understood and spoke English fairly well. We became quite fond of them and readily agreed to their suggestion to spend a few days at their station in Shekki, where they had a large orphanage. What a revelation that journey was to me. We had a day and a night's travel on the river steamer down the Pearl, certainly no joyride. Never in all my wildest imaginings could I have visualised anything so primitive. Along one side of the deck was a short, raised platform divided into narrow sections of two foot widths by a six inch high wooden partition.

Everyone slept here.

There were no beds or bed linen, just the board of the deck and a shaped metal object provided for the pillow, the idea being to rest one's neck on this. Sleep was impossible; the space allotted to each passenger was too narrow to turn over. It was, I should think, like lying in one's coffin.

We had plenty of entertainment, however, as the sounds were many and varied, from goats bleating, hens cackling and children crying, to the smacking of lips and burping from the crew, as they tucked into a meal that seemed far superior to the one offered us earlier in the day.

The smells I will leave to your imagination; sufficient to say that the toilet (one only) was full and foul as everyone pushed and fought to get in. A nice, well-educated Chinese gentleman occupied the bed space next to mine. He too was unable to sleep, so together we utilised the long hours of the night by studying some of the intricacies of the language.

The next morning, we were given water to wash, which we had to do before a crowd of spectators and still in the same confined space where we slept. We were served breakfast, consisting of rice and vegetables. Sitting cross-legged, in true Chinese style, using chopsticks, I felt I was fast becoming a national myself.

During our stay in Shekki, we had the privilege of attending a high-class wedding. The bridegroom was from a wealthy and influential family in Shekki and the bride, (betrothed to him since childhood) straight from the United States. What a glorious fascinating mixture of ancient and modern as well as East and West that was. The wedding took place in the ancestral hall with the magistrate of the city officiating.

The bride, defying the custom of traditional red, looked radiant in a white gown and veil and the handsome bridegroom, resplendent in top hat and tails, could have been mistaken for a Westerner. The sisters-in-law, however, who accompanied the bride — seven of them — were in customary red, their full-length richly embroidered dresses in stark contrast to the bridal white.

I was greatly intrigued to note that instead of confetti there were literally hundreds of fire crackers strung together and laced around the doors and windows of this vast hall. At a given signal and as the bride and groom emerged from the building these were ignited, with a resultant deafening noise that continued, it seemed, for hours until the smoke hung like a pall over the greater part of the city, scaring away the devils, they said.

One thousand guests attended the reception and as the only foreigners we were the guests of honour, sharing a table with the magistrate and his wife. What an initiation into Chinese food. Although the most expensive dishes, (rare delicacies) were served, mass cooking spoiled an otherwise delectable meal.

I was repulsed at the sight of shark fins spilling over the sides of the dish; and the octopus was so tough that it was impossible to break it into small pieces with chopsticks. Consequently in endeavouring to swallow a large piece of it, I almost choked. Miss Hewitt pushed me under the table to get rid of the offending piece as best I could and thankfully the scavenger dogs, hanging around with lean hungry looks, soon disposed of it. Let me hasten to add that normally the Chinese are wonderful cooks and their food, in my opinion, is the best in the world.

The life of the boat people in Canton was so full of interest that it merits a mention here. Looking onto the River Pearl from where we were staying we saw a ceaseless movement of boats, which literally covered its surface: huge junks laden with vegetables, smaller junks with huge sails suspended ,giving a most picturesque appearance. There were gaily coloured river steamers, sampans, (meaning three boards) of all sizes and descriptions and other craft.

Approximately nine tenths of these boats were inhabited by entire families who rarely set foot ashore, and when they did were easily recognisable by their rolling gait. There were barbers, carpenters, shoemakers, fortune tellers and boat stores selling every conceivable thing, in fact, a floating city, as complete in itself as anything on land.

The women and even the children were expert boatmen, steering their own sampan in and out among the maze of other craft without any mishap. In such limited surroundings babies were born, lived their lives, and died without knowing anything more than the confines of a small boat. I remember hearing of one mother whose baby at crawling stage, was tied by a length of rope to her own waist. When the baby fell overboard, as happened occasionally, the mother, feeling the tug of warning would haul the baby out of the water and into the boat again.

For a living they carried passengers backwards and forwards from one side of the river to the other. Miss Hewitt and I had quite a few adventures in crossing over.

One time, in a gale when the sampan we were in was overloaded and the high wind caused it to rock in a most alarming manner, we owed it to the skill of the two boys who rowed us across that we didn't experience a cold bath.

One Sunday morning, crossing over to the mainland for a Service, we took on board a passenger from another sampan which was seriously overloaded and looked about ready to sink. We hadn't long rescued him when the stubborn boatman, still struggling valiantly to reach the shore, had to jump for his life: just in time too as the boat plus its freight slowly disappeared beneath the surface of the water.

We were delighted to see among the river craft a Gospel boat, fully equipped for holding meetings. What a thrill Sunday mornings and evenings to see quite a number of the boat people rowing over to the Services! They too responded to the call of Christ, and began a new life in Him.

Our bookings for the plane were finalised just a few days before Christmas. We flew into Kunming on a transport plane, utilitarian rather than comfortable, with two metal seats running the length of the plane for passengers' use and the luggage stacked down the middle. We didn't mind the bumpy journey; it was just good to be on the move again and within hours of our final destination.

On our arrival brothers Wood, Colley, Savage and Francis were at the airport to meet us. They quickly got us through the formalities, then home to Lu-Shui-Ho (meaning Green Water). What excitement there was, everyone talking at once. How good to be among our own countrymen again, to chat away in English and be understood.

We listened spellbound to Mr Colley's graphic account of their adventures bringing the luggage by road. It was all safely to hand and waiting for us to unpack. I really looked forward to rummaging in my boxes.

It was wonderful to have arrived, delightful to see the children too, the two-year-old Savage twins and their seven-year-old brother who gave us a great welcome. How lovely they all were.

7

Language Problems in Kunming

The ancient city of Kunming, the capital of Yunnan province, is a very fascinating place, full of interest. It is situated on a plateau 6,000 ft above sea level, which gives it an ideal semitropical climate. One of its outstanding attractions is the great lake, a waterway to many of the beauty spots and to the lovely hills that surround the city.

Here again there was a glorious mixture of ancient and modern. The main streets were wide and tree lined, with beautiful shops and restaurants. On the other hand the side streets were narrow and dirty. There were open sewers attracting and breeding an abundance of flies and mosquitoes.

It was badly lit at night, so as a result we only ever frequented the main streets, which with the happy, jostling, good-natured crowds were a constant attraction. The buying and selling, the good-humoured bargaining, the many tea-houses where men would sit for hours drinking the Chinese green tea and listening to the famous story tellers, all added to the setting.

As was the fascinating sight and sound of the vibrating wire, ping-ping-ping as it cleaned and separated the cotton for use in mattresses, (or pukais, as they were commonly called in China). Beautiful ornate gates spanned the streets to the north, south, east and west.

Rickshaws, horse carts and quite a number of bicycles were seen on the streets, but seldom a car. Shops of the same kind were housed together and the streets named after the merchandise they sold, e.g. Silver Street, China Street, Straw Street. I was particularly fascinated to see how cleverly the artisans with tiny hammers and fine chisels engraved the most intricate patterns on silver plates and vases.

The ingenuity of the Chinese people was also marvellously portrayed in the variety of articles they produced out of bamboo and cane, ranging from hats, baskets and furniture to fans and fire blowers.

The smell of Chinese food pervaded the place and was so appetising that we were often tempted to go out and buy "Pao-tzers", a spiced meat dumpling, or maybe a bowl of Chinese noodles. It was even possible to buy ices in one particular ice cream bar. But when after a visit to this soda fountain we were all taken ill, we decided against buying any more.

Lu-Shui-Hu (Green Water Pond) was now our

missionary home, so called because of its close proximity to a green slimy pond. It was a big house with 32 rooms with an outer and inner courtyard. It was typically Chinese with its curved roofs, verandas and moongate. Mr Colley was gradually equipping each room with more modern furniture, and it was very comfortable. I look back with pleasure on my first six months there.

Mrs Colley — Wynne, we called her — was a lovely housemother, making it home for every one of us.

The street calls took some getting used to. I was awakened regularly around 1:30 a.m. by a raucous voice, which sounded almost directly underneath my window, shouting *"Kai-men"* (Open the door) over and over again.

There were frequent rows, too. The policeman had his box just outside the house, and quarrels and fights were usually settled there. The early morning calls were tiresome when we wanted to sleep, but amusing nevertheless. The paper man shouting out the names of the daily papers, the water seller *(Ho Shiui)*, some offering flea medicine *(Pai-tzu-yo)*, or eggs *(chi-dan)* and countless others. There were various sounds in the night too that were disturbing, to say the least.

Squirrel rats were a nuisance. They got between the roof and ceiling and made a terrible clatter. Then there were the frogs in the pond. I wouldn't like to hazard a guess, but it sounded like hundreds of them croaking all night.

The common-type rats, too, were plentiful. I remember them almost the size of cats climbing in and out of the waste bin near the kitchen in broad daylight, while the men had a bit of sport, shooting at them with air rifles.

Our water was drawn from the well in the first courtyard and I remember that it tasted foul. It had to be drained not long afterwards, when they found a couple of dead animals at the bottom.

I was curious to hear the missionaries talking about the scent bottles, wondering what on earth they were. I soon found out after following behind them one morning. Once or twice a week, someone would come and empty our toilet (privy-midden). They paid us for this as it made good fertile soil. This was carried through the streets in two large baskets, suspended by a pole over the shoulders of a coolie. Follow him once and you did not wish to repeat the experience.

Just a word here about our "toilet", which was a constant source of amusement. Situated at the bottom of the long garden and reached by a narrow path from the house, there was no way of knowing if it was occupied or vacant and rather embarrassing to walk all the way down the path, in view of the dining room and sitting room, and have to turn away disappointed.

Mr Wood, however, had a brilliant idea. He made a big wooden ball with a metal attachment, which was left on a window sill in the inner courtyard, the idea being to take it with you and return it afterwards. This was very successful until one day a certain missionary found himself in a rickshaw going to the bank, with the ball still in his possession.

After this incident it ceased to be called the "ballroom", but became known as the "lighthouse", when Mr Colley fixed an electric light, which was switched on when going down the path, and off on returning.

Language study soon engaged my full attention and I found it really fascinating, though the possibility of some day preaching in it seemed remote. However having a good memory was a tremendous help. There was no alphabet, but there was a good Primer arranged by a fellow called Baller, who had done an excellent job in putting the language into a sort of grammar. With the aid of this and with the help of Mrs Wood's adopted daughter Chen-Li, who patiently taught me, I slowly but surely began to learn this difficult language.

Putting it into practice though was more difficult. The Mandarin Chinese with its five tones and spoken by two-thirds of the population of China, had all newcomers and sometimes more experienced missionaries in despair, as repeated mistakes were made in the wrong use of tones. One particular preacher, I remember, called down water instead of fire on Elijah's sacrifice at Carmel.

It speaks well for the Chinese that they not only overlooked our outrageous mistakes but endeavoured to understand what we were trying to say. Fortunately, in preaching, the context gave the clue. I looked forward tremendously to the day when, instead of a confused jumble of sounds and characters, it would begin to make sense. In the meantime I attended services and tried to look intelligent, though I found listening to an hour's message in a language I didn't understand very trying. Playing the piano accordion helped to pass the time, however, and there was often some unusual thing happening in the services, but I remember times of terrible frustration. I think the language barrier was as much a trial to the Chinese as it was to me. They would crowd around, all trying to shake hands at once and if I made the fatal mistake of trying out one or two words already familiar, it would be met with a barrage of language, spoken fast and loud that left me stupefied.

The Kunming church was large, seating between 200 and 300 people. To see this hall crowded was an inspiring sight. The services were very different from those in the homeland. The people sang with abandon, though quite tunelessly most of the time. There was a constant coming and going, sometimes the whole congregation changing once or even twice during the course of the meeting. Mothers openly fed their babies, children ran around in the nude, while some of the little ones relieved themselves, though this was frowned upon by our pastor.

Dogs would wander in and be noisily removed, and there was usually plenty of noise and scuffling of feet. It seemed strange to see the men wearing trilby hats all through the service (they were so proud of them). The older women wore the traditional Chinese blue, but the girls and younger women looked pretty in bright, floral gowns.

There was no set time for the service to finish; it depended on the preacher — and some of them never knew when to stop. One old gentleman I remember began his message in Genesis at the 'Fall of man' and slowly and systematically went through the Bible. I made my exit just as he was giving the account of David's fight with Goliath, my patience completely exhausted.

In spite of many interruptions and the disadvantage of preaching to a moving congregation, the Gospel message winged its way into the hearts of many, and lives were transformed by the mighty power of God.

The Chinese were known as the black haired race, and without exception they all had that marvellous blue-black hair and dark eyes, which I found very attractive. So we foreigners with our red, brown, or blond hair and eyes of different colours, were quite a curiosity. Our fair skin made it difficult for them to guess our age.

I remember an old woman lifting my dress to see if I was the same colour all over. And I heard another whisper to her neighbour, "She must be about one hundred; look at the colour of her hair!" We never went out without a crowd of followers, mainly children, but sometimes the adults were equally curious.

The names they called us were not very complimentary, *Kao-goo* (high noses), *Lao-yang-min* (old foreign bleating goat), etc.

Despite the strangeness, the desperate poverty, dirty houses and clothing of some of the folk; despite the narrow streets, the crowds, the mangy flea-bitten dogs and the open sewers, I was learning to love this place and to love the people.

About this time I joined up with the youth of our Kunming church. We had wonderful happy times together, picnicking by the lake and attending early morning prayer meetings in the park. Stephen Ko, one of the youth leaders who was a middle school teacher, spoke excellent English and was always ready to interpret for me. Two of the girls became my good friends. Although we could not converse much because of my still very limited Chinese, we somehow made ourselves understood with plenty of laughter of course.

From then I knew real joy and contentment and with their continual help, I experienced the added thrill of seeing the language open up to me.

A word about rickshaws; one of the most relaxing things I know is to take a ride in a rickshaw, particularly if the coolie is strong and tough and able to pull at a brisk pace. Bowling along the streets in this way gives one a wonderful feeling.

There were many amusing incidents. I remember the German missionaries telling of a colleague who had received notice of a remittance in the bank following the war, (the Germans had suffered extreme poverty during the war years as no funds were available to them; but for the help of the American Red Cross, they would probably have starved) so it was with great excitement that this rather stout lady took a rickshaw to the bank. The waiting coolie, standing loosely holding the shafts, didn't notice her exuberant return until she bounced into the rickshaw, tilting it backwards and shooting the unsuspecting coolie up into the air, still holding on to the shafts. The scene was hilarious as each shouted at the other, the lady wanting to get up and he, in spite of furious kicking of his legs, unable to bring himself down. The crowd who gathered were too helpless with laughter to be of any assistance.

Mr Colley also told us of an amusing incident when he took a rickshaw to the bank. Being in a hurry, the coolie was running at quite a spanking pace, warning the folk out of the way with the frequent use of a little bell attached to one of the shafts. A mulish sort of fellow refused to budge in spite of frequent warnings, so the rickshaw coolie calmly caught him between the shafts in front, so forcing him to run all the way to the bank too, now and then giving him a kick to urge him on!

I was shocked one day, riding down the main street of Kunming, to hear my rickshaw coolie call out to his colleague on the opposite side of the street, "What do you think of this big fat old pig that I've got here?" I didn't get the other's reply, but as his passenger was a stout old gentleman, I doubt whether it was any more complimentary.

All this had to be taken in good part, as it was considered "bad breeding" to lose one's temper. "Face" or self respect was very important to the Chinese. They were a proud and courteous people, showing consideration for an individual's feelings. This was one of their great virtues and they appreciated consideration of theirs too. I noticed they didn't criticise each other as frankly as we do. They also highly respect their old people and listen to their advice.

I found it was unforgivable to make a Chinese person lose face. It was far better and safer to lose face oneself than make an enemy for life. I had one or two unfortunate encounters with them before I learned this lesson.

On one occasion, Mrs Wood, Yin-Chen and I planned a visit to Fumin, where Miss Hewitt was then working. We were going by horse-cart but had to take a rickshaw as far as the City Gates. It was a wet day and the roads were filthy. Arriving at the starting place for the horse-carts I paid the coolies, offering them the amount we had agreed, but they insisted we had settled for a higher price. I knew this was quite wrong of course and had been warned about this very thing, and not to yield to their wishes. They refused what I offered them, however, and threw the paper notes on the ground, where they were trodden into the mud by passers-by. It was a battle of wills. I stubbornly refused to give any more and they, with raised voices and a stream of language that I couldn't understand, would not budge an inch either.

The crowds were gathering around us, very curious to see how it would end, and not one of them willing to take the "foreign devil's" part. Eventually we had to go up to the Police box for a settlement. The young policeman kindly listened to what I had to say. I think he knew I was right, but in order to prevent the coolies losing face, he made me pay, not only what they demanded, but in clean notes too.

On another occasion, I took the three Colley children for a day across the lake. Mr Colley had not been well and he and his wife were spending a few days over there. We had booked a sampan for the return journey, and were about to push off from the shore to return home, when a young Chinese fellow jumped in. We had a very rough crossing, the children were sick and miserable and this young fellow was very helpful; holding their heads, cleaning the vomit from their clothes and at the same time talking to me in rapid Chinese, which was beyond my level of comprehension at the time. I was only able to manage a few elementary sentences, and because I was feeling so wretched myself, answered all his questions in the affirmative, as an easy way out.

Arriving at the landing stage in Kunming, with the children sick and tired on a wet dark night, I was delighted when the young man offered to get the rickshaw needed. But instead of leaving us there, he ran alongside my rickshaw all the way back to "Lu-shui-hu". Nor could we get rid of him. He insisted on coming into the compound, telling our missionaries that he was now my boy and that I had engaged him to cook and to look after my home and children! I was flabbergasted — but it seemed I had said yes to his request to be my servant.

What a job we had to make him go. Finally we got the matter settled with the police at the corner. The result being that I had to pay him one month's wages before he would go, and to prevent him losing face.

I was very wary after this, making sure that in all business transactions we not only understood each other, but parted good friends.

It has been jokingly said, there are 999 different smells in China. There are certainly quite a few, but one of the prevailing smells that initially nauseated me and was on everyone's breath, in fact seemed to ooze out of their pores, was the smell of "*chu-tsai*" (garlic). It was virtually unknown in Britain at that time, but we were told that the only way to counteract this was to eat it ourselves. This was certainly no hardship, for we all loved Chinese food and when we knew Ting-szu-fu, our cook, was preparing one for our midday meal, we could scarcely wait until the dinner gong sounded.

We looked forward tremendously to those occasional times when we were invited out to a feast. This could mean anything from twenty to thirty dishes, each one more delectable than the one before. Starting with the cold dish for instance, a plate of small delicate portions of roast duck and chicken, neatly rolled portions of ham, sliced hard-boiled eggs and tomatoes, nuts, beef and pork, so beautifully cooked and delightfully arranged that one had to exercise great will-power not to continue eating this first dish. This was only the start, however; there were many more tasty and appetising dishes to follow.

The fish was brought in on a large platter; the head and skin complete, as Chinese like their fish cooked whole and as someone said, "There is a wonderful delicate taste about these fish-heads!" We however felt slightly hypnotised by the stony stare of a reproachful fish eye. The special sauce which covered the fish was one of the Chinese culinary arts and tasted really delicious.

Then there was "Bombing Tokyo!" This dish of succulent pork, sizzling in the most appetising sauce, was so piping hot, that it was bursting with small popping sounds ... We were served whole chicken cooked in rare spices; pork dishes; vegetables of all kinds; pickled walnuts, and other dishes too mysterious to be identified.

No wonder we staggered home so replete that we didn't even want to talk.

Ruth with her two special friends

8

Challenges at Niliang

Six months after my arrival in Kunming, I sat my first language examination. Having passed with honours, I was now ready for action.

It had been decided that I should join Miss Brown, who was then working in the city of Niliang, a place directly on the railway route from the capital and a four-hour journey away.

This scenic railway was a marvellous feat of engineering. Cutting right through the mountains, it afforded breathtaking views. The journey over one stretch, I remember, was a nerve-racking ordeal, as we appeared to be suspended over abysmal ravines. Another part of the journey took us through a tunnel so long and narrow that even with windows closed we were almost suffocated by the fumes.

Arriving at Niliang, we hired coolies to take the

luggage, and to celebrate our arrival took sedan chairs ourselves. We felt like royalty as we were borne high on the shoulders of the carriers, skirting the paddy fields and wending our way through the crowded streets of the city. Everyone stopped work to wave us a greeting, and the children followed all the way, shouting with excitement.

It was quite a journey and I had plenty of opportunity to gaze around at my new home. We had a wonderful view of the picturesque city wall, stretching up into the hills to the South Gate and dipping down to the plains at the North Gate.

The city itself was quite small, with narrow streets and ancient buildings. Garbage and litter covered the sidewalks. Scavenger dogs seemed to be everywhere, and the open sewers bordering the streets filled the hot air with obnoxious smells.

The Mission and Gospel Hall building was outside the city, as was half the population. This was no disadvantage except when there was trouble. The gates were then locked at dusk, leaving those of us who lived outside the city walls with a sense of isolation.

The Gospel Hall was a converted shop on one of the main streets and we had our living quarters above. It was a very old building, typically Chinese in architecture, with its rooms built around an open courtyard and a small garden to the rear.

What fun we had, transforming this old Chinese house into an English home, brightening the dark rooms and hiding the ugly woodwork with pretty curtains.

My *er fang* (Ear Room), a long, narrow side room was soon transformed into a bower with white muslin curtains and drapes, pretty cushions and bedcovers; as dainty a room as any girl could wish for and my beauty-loving soul was satisfied.

I soon made my acquaintance with the Christians. Li-da-ma, our Bible woman, was a tall dignified person who spoke in a quiet, gentle voice but was firm and resolute in her stand for righteousness. Chang-da-sal, a little woman who lived just on the other side of the street, was one of those indispensable helpers, willing and ready to do anything. Chien-da-sal, our girl who cooked, washed and cleaned for us, was industrious and hard working but always cheerful. I grew to love them all.

One of the godly men I met was Cho-Hsien-seng. He had been an evangelist for years and still loved to preach in spite of advancing years. He made a quaint figure as he stood to preach on the Sunday morning, his blue faded gown reaching down to his feet, revealing a pair of shabby Chinese cloth slippers. A couple of decayed teeth saved him from being absolutely toothless, (there was no way for the poorer folk in China to replace their rotting teeth — they just fell out and necessary adjustments had to be made with food). A few white wisps of hair helped to cover an otherwise bald head and he fondled lovingly the few straggly hairs that made up his beard. The Chinese men were smooth faced and seldom sported a beard, so Cho-Hsien-seng was very proud of his. Standing to preach the Gospel, however, he assumed a new dignity, even though he emphasised his points with the flourish of a back-scratcher, used occasionally to scratch his back.

Another great character was Tong-da-di, one of those bright, breezy fellows. Always the first to arrive at a meeting, he would sit on the front row and enjoy every minute of the service. He couldn't sing a note in tune and although we pointed out every character on the hymn sheet as we sang, he always managed to be a line or two behind the others.

I remember well the night he caught fire!

In the colder months of the year, the older Christians would carry a fire basket around with them and stand it between their feet during the service — a great comfort, as I myself experienced. Tong-da-di, however, liked his basket between his knees, under his long gown, thus conserving every bit of heat. On this particular evening his fire basket proved too hot, and smoke began to pour out of the neck of his gown to his consternation and the amusement of the rest of the congregation. He was actually on fire.

He wasn't hurt, however, and we soon had the fire out. Peace and order were restored.

There was also Suen-da-di, a tall thin man, who was never seen in the Gospel Hall without his little china teapot, from which he periodically regaled himself during the course of the service.

So many more I could mention, and I grew to love them all: toothless old grannies, children, youths and men and women of such a variety of personalities. My life became bound up in them as I learned to appreciate the contribution that each made to our fellowship.

Our day began very early in the morning with

prayer for anyone who could get along to the Fu-Yin-Tang (Gospel Hall) and this could mean any time after dawn, for there were very few clocks and watches around. The Chinese usually got up when it was light and went to bed at dark.

Eight or nine of these friends gathered each morning and the strains of the first hymn would warn us of their arrival.

I had it easy in the beginning as my language was not yet fluent, but after passing my second exam, I plunged fully into the work and this quarter of an hour's message each morning, whilst somewhat exacting because of a heavy syllabus for my third and last exam, was marvellous language practice nevertheless.

We were kept busy all day and every day.

Niliang, although not a big city in itself, had 365 villages on the plain and these too came under our care. We endeavoured to visit each one once or twice a year. Consequently we had a very heavy programme. It meant a lot of walking from village to village, with an open air meeting in each place and the distribution of tracts to every family.

Many of the villages in the remote valleys were isolated from the outside world. The people kept their own pigs and chickens, and were simple, kindly folk. I personally loved these days out.

Starting off first thing in the morning with our Bible woman and someone to carry the piano accordion, and equipped with food and plenty of drink, we were set for the day. As our route invariably led us through the paddy fields, we were fascinated to watch the farmers using all kinds of ingenious methods in the ploughing and harvesting of their crops, and the ever-changing complexity of the countryside never failed to give us pleasure.

First of all the plains were flooded with water, allowing the dry scorched earth to be softened ready for the water buffalo who ploughed up the earth by tramping steadily up and down, guided skilfully by young boys, riding on wooden platforms, also drawn by the buffalo. The team spirit then came into action, as men and women of all ages, with children too, worked systematically right across the plains, transplanting the tender rice shoots.

Every day for weeks they would stand, often above their knees in water, rapidly pushing the shoots into the softened earth. One of the loveliest sights is the fresh green of the young rice.

The Harvest was a great occasion, when with that same marvellous team effort, they would work every field, beginning at the furthermost point of the plain and advancing slowly toward the city itself. This brought the crowds into Niliang and we, to whom was committed the eternal seed, made good use of the occasion by holding special services, when by the grace of God, and the help of His Spirit, we were privileged to see a little of the great eternal harvest.

Alternating with the rice was the cultivation of the broad bean. The lovely fragrance of this plant in flower penetrated even as far as the city streets. Indeed, all these years later, I still have nostalgic memories of the intoxicating scent.

As we approached our first village, already the children had spotted us and heralded our arrival with shouts that filled the air. "Jesus is coming, the *Wai-gou-ren* (foreigners) are here." Soon every dog in the village had joined in the chorus. The women dropped what they were doing and ran out to meet us and the men sauntered up.

As we fixed our hymn sheet on the wall of one of the buildings and began to sing one of our well-loved Gospel hymns, they gathered round.

There were still villages, of course, that were completely unreached, where they believed that we gouge out babies' eyes to make medicine, and were in mortal terror of the white man. But thank God they were few and far between. On the whole we were accepted and our message listened to. True, we were objects of wonder to them, from the soles of our feet to the crown of our head. They pinched us to see if our skin felt like theirs. Our eyes and hair fascinated them, but when we started to preach in their language, so that they understood, the smiles began to break out on their faces and they listened intently to the sweet story of salvation. Our reward was the joy of leading some of them to the Saviour.

Not long after my arrival in Niliang, I accompanied Miss Brown to the leper colony where she had started a very needy ministry among the lepers.

Walking through the paddy fields together that day, and up into the hills where the leper colony was situated, a journey of six or seven miles, she told me an interesting story of how this work began. I pass it on to you as she told me.

Miss Brown's story:
One day our Chinese evangelist was making his way back to Niliang from a preaching visit at some distant village, and in taking a short cut over the

hills, he saw tucked away in the hollow and completely isolated, what appeared to be an old derelict building.

His curiosity piqued, he walked over to see if anyone lived in it. But when he peered through the big iron moongate, which was securely padlocked on the outside, the place seemed utterly deserted. After shouting loudly a few times, he was surprised to see crawling toward the gate on all fours, what appeared at first sight to be some sort of animal. He was amazed to find it was a man, so terribly deformed and disfigured as to be almost unrecognisable.

The evangelist enquired who he was and what he was doing there, and was shocked to hear that there were twenty or more lepers locked up in that old Chinese building.

"No one comes to see us or bring us any food; we are left here to die," one said. "When we get too many they take us out on the hillside and shoot us, or else dig a big hole and bury us alive. We have no one to care for us."

When the evangelist came back to the Gospel Hall and told this sad story, Miss Brown immediately went to the magistrate of the city and asked his permission to visit the lepers and help them. God gave her favour with this man. He not only gave her permission to visit them, but promised to provide two sacks of rice every month.

So began a new life, in every sense of the word for the lepers of Niliang. Those who were able were encouraged to dig and cultivate the ground all around the building. They were given seed and vegetable plants, and within a short time were able to gather their own produce.

More wonderful still, as the Gospel was preached week by week, they responded to the claims of Christ and became Christian men and women.

As we climbed the hills and drew nearer to our destination, the countryside became more wild and rugged; civilisation seemed to be left far behind.

Arriving at the top of the last and steepest hill, I had my first glimpse of the colony, lying in the hollow, nestling among the hills; it appeared as a green oasis in an otherwise barren spot.

Fruit trees were in abundance and formed a lovely leafy bower right to the door of the place. Sugar cane, bananas and papaya seemed plentiful; and there must have been every kind of vegetable growing here.

As soon as we stepped through the gate there was a brisk "One, two, three..." from their leader, a former middle school teacher, and together the lepers sang a song of welcome, tuneless but so sincere that it brought a lump to my throat.

How can I describe that touching scene as they tried to show their gratitude for our coming. Some of them were in a lamentable state; one dear woman whose face was practically destroyed by this loathsome disease had tied a handkerchief around it to hide it from our gaze.

Great leprous sores covered their bodies, making them repulsive to look at; hands and feet were crippled, their clothes ragged and torn and the place they had to call home was so cheerless and desolate, it brought tears to my eyes.

What a great message we had for them in their dire need. Our hearts rejoiced to see the enthusiasm with which they sang the hymns and listened to the word of God. Their only hope was in accepting Jesus as Saviour, and praise God, every one of them gladly did just that.

Once or twice a week we visited them, treating their sores and giving them the necessary injections. We were overjoyed to see their health improving in a wonderful way even to the discharging of one or two.

Their regular diet and treatment helped tremendously in combating the disease, but the greatest thrill to us was to know that they all belonged to Christ.

One day a distracted mother brought her daughter-in-law to the Gospel Hall. Delivered of her first baby, a fine and coveted grandson for the mother-in-law ten days ago, she had developed a severe rash which practically covered her whole body. Miss Brown took a blood sample, promising to let the mother-in-law know the result as soon as possible. Two days later, we heard that the girl, just 17 years of age, had been taken to the leper colony, her baby rudely snatched from her arms. I will never forget the stricken look on that girl's face when we saw her a few days later.

She would not accept the fact that she was a leper, refusing to sit with any of the others and using her own cooking and eating utensils. But although the rash disappeared and she looked perfectly normal for a time, unfortunately the germ was in her bloodstream and I saw her change from a pretty young girl to someone who was ugly and deformed as the disease took its full toll.

How rightly leprosy has been used as a picture of

sin, crippling and destroying in its devastating action in the souls of men and women, blighting and marring young lives. Thank God there is a remedy and this was our mission: to present our Lord Jesus who came to seek and to save as well as heal, that which was lost.

Miss Brown moved shortly afterwards to another station, but together with one of our Christian women, I continued to visit the lepers regularly and with funds now available from the National Leprosy Campaign in the United States, was able to give them more up-to-date treatment, and more importantly, to minister to their souls.

The appalling living conditions at the Colony, however, hindered us in our efforts to heal those dreadful sores, as was evidenced on one occasion when I had to make a surprise visit the day following my weekly treatment.

Imagine my amazement and my chagrin too, to find all their bandages off and the sores if anything in a worse condition. They told me then what had happened. During the night, while they slept the rats, in an attempt to get at the ointment which they liked, had torn away the bandages, gnawing at the sores. The lepers were quite unaware of this because of the insensitivity of the affected limbs.

Until I left China, rather abruptly because of the Communist takeover some two years later, the weekly walk through the paddy fields and up to the leper colony was one of my favourite activities. I came to know every one of those dear folk intimately and there was mutual love and understanding. Little by little I was enabled by special funds to make their life a little easier. They were each given a mattress, towels and soap, cloth to make into garments, salt — a precious commodity, and occasionally as a special treat, some meat. The joy on their faces was all the thanks I needed.

Dr Chang, the elder of our Niliang church, was a fine Christian gentleman with a lovely wife and children. In a quiet, unassuming way he did a lot of good in the city. Realising the need of some help for the distressed maternity cases he had opened a small midwifery hospital, though he himself didn't feel competent enough to tackle any abnormal cases. So I was asked to help; but what a formidable task, totally out of my province as a midwife.

I had never applied forceps to a baby's head, though I had often helped with forceps deliveries. I knew all the theory of manual removal of the placenta, but dreaded the thought of doing one myself.

Here was a need, however, and the promise was right there in the Book: *"For I can do all things through Christ, who strengthens me".* (Phil 4:13) (NKJV)

This surely was one of these "all things". Dare I take Him at His word and launch out on this promise? With a trembling heart, I made my decision.

He had never failed me yet, wasn't this an opportunity to prove His mighty power?

Some weeks later I walked through the silent streets in the middle of the night in answer to a hospital call, which would undoubtedly mean life or death for mother or baby, or both. My teeth chattered as I contemplated what might be waiting for me. In the ensuing drama, enacted in that primitive maternity hospital, I experienced in a very real way the Lord standing by me, answering my silent cry for help, with wonderful success.

The joy of that moment defies description: the baby's lusty cry; the happy tears of the mother; the relief in all our hearts and then the walk back through the awakening city with buoyant step and a deep sense of gratitude to Him who never fails.

The days passed into weeks and the weeks into months. Miss Knell returned to Niliang, her own station, after a long absence of illness and furlough. The people gave her as enthusiastic a welcome as any queen.

It was a delight to hear her preach in Chinese smoothly and easily as any of the nationals, and I learned much from her great store of wisdom and knowledge in the months that followed.

I had now acquired two good Chinese friends. Shui-Shen, a pretty young postgraduate, now married and settled in Niliang, and Xi-Cheng-Ching, our landlady's youngest son with whom I was studying Chinese in exchange for half-an-hour's English conversation. In our free evenings we had delightful walks up into the hills, visiting the many pagodas and temples. It never failed to astound me that intelligent, well-educated people could bow down and worship the grotesque idols we saw in these places. Hideously painted in garish colours of red, blue, yellow and gold, pot bellied and pop eyed, these monsters would surely strike terror into any child's heart.

The many-armed goddess of mercy and the three-headed idol that grinned hideously down on us, were only two of the hundreds of ugly images that we saw. There were thousands of such temples, found all over China where the people, rich and poor, educated and ignorant, offered their prayers, burned their incense and made their oblations.

The prevalence of idol worship was manifested in the little shrines set in the hillsides, and in the family altars in most homes, where the old *tai-tai* (mother) would make her offering every morning before doing anything else; a bowl of peanuts or a few pomegranates, a handful of bananas or even just a bowlful of rice. In most homes we would see the endless paper idols, stuck on walls and doors.

The ancestral worship too, was something in which every Chinese person participated. Speaking with Xi-Cheng-Ching one day concerning this very thing, I was amazed to find that he believed in it profoundly, offering his worship with the rest, even though he was well educated, westernised in dress and spoke good English.

The Chinese New Year was a great occasion, when old debts were paid off, quarrels settled, houses swept and decorated, old paper idols taken down and replaced by new ones, in fact a complete new start made. I suppose, in a less exaggerated way, we in the Western countries do the same sort of thing in turning over a new leaf at New Year.

The dancing of the dragon in the Lantern Festival was fascinating to watch. For thousands of years the dragon had been the emblem of China and though it was not worshipped now so fervently, it still was very much in evidence. Displayed on ships, posters and scrolls and painted on the oiled paper sunshades and fans, it still captured the people's imagination, particularly on the night of the Lantern Festival. At this festival many orange and red lanterns, joined in sections to form the body of a serpent, were carried section by section, so that the snake-like effect of twisting and turning was easily simulated.

The head was made of coloured paper, supported by bamboo strips, and was manipulated by one of the men, while someone else had a large paper ball, which dangled in a tantalising way before the dragon. When this long 40 ft or more length of dragon was lit up and seen at night, bobbing up and down, twisting and turning along the roads through the towns and villages and up over the hillside, it looked as realistic as any movie monster. To watch the men make it dance and catch the paper ball in its mouth, was a feat for which the folk gladly paid their money.

In the face of all this idolatry it was thrilling to see the Gospel Hall filled with believers each meeting, worshipping our wonderful Lord. This ordinary little shop that had been converted into a preaching chapel, with its rough benches and heavy glassless wooden window frames, had become the very gate of heaven for so many of them. As soon as the shutters were removed and the doors opened, the people would flock in; while many more would crowd around the windows listening.

Some of them, not wishing to be seen, would hide behind the wooden frames, but intently listening nevertheless. It was interesting to see their evident progress as the Spirit began to move upon their hearts. Coming out from their hiding place, they would stand leaning on the boards of the windows, then perhaps a week or two later, we would find them sitting on the back row inside.

Slowly, as the Word worked in their hearts, they would move up seat by seat, until with faces alight with pure joy, we would find them at the front, worshipping with the rest of God's family.

Just when they made their decision it was difficult to know, nor did it matter really; somewhere between the back row and the front they were spiritually born again, as was evidenced by the change in their lives.

Life for most of the inhabitants of Niliang was meagre and hard; they eked out a living from the sale of a few oranges, eggs and such like, content with their one or two meals of rice and vegetables each day. The clothes they wore were so well patched that it was difficult to tell the original piece.

Most of the older women had the tiny bound feet of their generation, though the cruel custom had now been abolished and the younger women were happy to have normal healthy feet. Strange as it may seem, many of the young men preferred the tiny bound feet to the big feet of the younger girls.

There were the more delicate and cultured women of wealthier class, with their glossy well-groomed hair and finely chiselled faces. I sometimes had the privilege of delivering them of their babies, but on the whole our work of making disciples was among the peasant class. And has it not always been so, so that in Christ's day, it was said: *"the common people heard Him gladly."* (Mark 12:37)

In spite of generations of civilisation and a culture that had been the greatest in the world, it was a society with a crude and barbaric side. I was aghast at the cruel way they treated their mules, beating them mercilessly until there were open sores on their backs. Sometimes the animal would slip on the cobblestones and fall down under its heavy load, but instead of helping it to get up, they would beat it until it staggered to its feet.

I can never forget the horror of seeing the recently severed head of a bandit, hanging by its hair over the gate of the city, still dripping blood on the cobblestones beneath. Nor the suspicious bundles suspended from the trees or flung away in the bushes for the animals and birds to devour — which we were told were unwanted baby girls.

One evening while Miss Knell was preaching in the Gospel Hall, to my indignation a small boy stooped in the aisle and defecated, watched indifferently by his mother. When I remonstrated with her, she looked at me coolly, sauntered to the door and called in one of the scavenger dogs, which quickly cleared up the mess.

Dogs ran wild in China. They were mangy, flea ridden and never fed. Seldom if ever kept as pets, they foraged their food wherever they could and multiplied at an alarming rate.

Cats, on the other hand, were kept on leads and were very precious pets. They were rarely seen on the streets and were practically impossible to buy, hence the plague of rats.

Miss Brown, however, kept three Siamese cats which she guarded jealously. Envious eyes had often been upon them, but they certainly kept the rats at bay.

Periodically, it became necessary to cut down on the dog population, but what an inhumane method they adopted. Two or three men were delegated to club them to death. Although this was done at dawn, before anyone was around, the yelps and howls of these unfortunate creatures filled the air and penetrated to every part of the city.

In this animal-loving country of ours, we read with horror of such things, but this was the reality of China at the time I was there.

The leper lady who covered her face with a handkerchief to hide the disfigurement

9

Troubled Times

The days passed, weeks merged into months and all unconsciously into years. There was the occasional trip to Kunming, the capital, to exchange money or buy in stores; happy little breaks in the routine, but I personally found great fulfilment in the varied activities of our busy life in Niliang.

The highlight of each week was my mother's letter. To know she was happy and well added zest to the engaging task of winning souls for Christ.

There was the long-awaited visit of our Overseas Mission Council brethren from England, Mr Donald Gee and Mr L.F. Woodward in October 1948. Pentecostal missionaries from every part of Yunnan province gathered in Kunming for a spiritual feast. I remember the weighty discussions we had in the conference days which followed.

The storm clouds of Communism were gathering over the whole of China, and we wondered how much longer we would be permitted to preach the Gospel.

As we saw our two visitors off on the next lap of their journey to India, and returned to our individual mission stations, it was with a new determination to push the battle to the gates and snatch as many souls for Christ as possible before the doors of China closed against us. It was now widely understood that the Communists were gathering their forces in the south of China, while much of the north was already in their hands.

Our opportunity was now or never.

Back in Niliang our heavy work schedule left little time for anything else. We had no newspapers, and for a short period had the unique experience of living without watch or clock of any description. We went to bed when the services were over, got up at dawn and ate when we were hungry. It worked very well on the whole, though one visitor found us having dinner at 10:30 in the morning!

It was after the disappointing experience, however, of missing the only train of the day to the capital that I decided to buy a watch.

From the windows of my *er-fang* overlooking the courtyard I could see all the comings and goings of the day. There were countless interruptions during my language study sessions and I had serious doubts as to whether I would ever be ready to sit my third language examination.

Someone would come in needing prayer; a mother with a sick child requiring medicine; our evangelist with a few problems; someone with family troubles, or maybe the interruption of a funeral procession passing by, the din and noise of firecrackers and the weeping and wailing of the white-clad mourners, genuine and professional. I always felt sorry for the sixteen or more men who carried the heavy wooden coffin, staggering under its weight and perspiring freely as the sun beat mercilessly upon them. The extravagant paper decorations which literally covered its ugly wooden structure gave a bizarre appearance.

1949 saw the arrival of a new missionary to the field. Idris Parry was a young Welshman from Brynmawr, Breconshire. Saved at the age of 18, he had served the Lord with unswerving devotion. The call to work in Tibet had been his goal for a number of years and it was with enthusiasm that he applied himself to language study.

At our Field Conference in October 1948 his photograph had been passed around for us to see and I remember two of our lady missionaries remarking to me that he would probably be my future husband. I laughed with them, not giving the matter a second thought. There was certainly no opportunity of developing a friendship. We were kept strictly apart except for one trip up to Kunming on business, when we were casually introduced. I never saw him again until we were all together selling what stuff we could to get our air fare out of China. Little did I know that my future and his were to become so closely entwined.

The ensuing months brought a sense of foreboding. Tension was mounting and events were speeding towards the inevitable climax.

There were one or two disturbing incidents in Niliang. Communist brigands were reported in the hills surrounding the city and the gates were locked at dusk.

One day four men and one woman, heavily manacled and roped together, were led around the streets for everyone to gaze at. They were brigands who had been caught just outside the city and were now to be executed. As Miss Knell and I appeared at the door of the Gospel Hall the woman cried out for us to intervene and save her. But we dared not interfere, except to tell her to believe in Jesus.

A few days later, returning from a midwifery case at the hospital, I found myself caught up in a crowd as they pushed and jostled their way to the *Ya-Men*. I was told the five culprits were facing a firing squad that morning. There was no escape. Jammed in the crowds, I was forced to witness this horrible scene as each one fell lifeless to the ground.

As I looked round at the faces of the people, I wondered if any of them was capable of showing mercy.

Several quiet, uneventful weeks passed and we endeavoured to keep up with village work and our regular weekly visit to the lepers, although there were a number of scares. Our Christian women were disturbed that I was going so far out from the city and among the hills, where they knew bands of robbers were lurking. I didn't feel any fear, however, and was often conscious of the angels of the Lord encamping around me.

Coming away from a village one day, we passed

a small group of youngish men who looked us over rather insolently, but didn't attempt to speak to us or detain us. Safely out of earshot, however, our Bible woman told me they were brigands from the hills. How she knew I don't know, but we did thank God for His loving care of us.

Returning from one of these preaching tours one day I found Miss Knell very unwell with a rising temperature. Dr Chang saw her but could not diagnose her illness. Each day her condition deteriorated, until I realised I would have to get her into hospital.

A hurried letter was sent off to Mr Holder, who was then in charge of the Kunming home, but I knew I couldn't expect any reply or help for two or three days. That evening Miss Knell lapsed into unconsciousness. It would be impossible to describe how desolate I felt as I realised the burden of responsibility.

Towards evening some of the elders of the church and the women came with the news that the brigands were only a mile and a half from the city and intended breaking into Niliang during the night. They said I must get away immediately and take Miss Knell to Kunming, as the Gospel Hall was to be the first place of attack. Unfortunately we were outside the walls of the city and therefore utterly without natural protection, but He who never slumbers or sleeps was again in command of the situation.

Knowing how impossible it was to think of moving Miss Knell, they prayed with me, committing us both to God's loving care, and left.

After tending to her and doing all I could to make

her comfortable for the night, I too lay down, resting my heart on that wonderful promise in Psalm 4:8: *"In peace I will lie down and sleep, for You alone, O Lord, will keep me safe."*

There was plenty of gunfire and shouting during the night, but I slept and woke the next morning to find Miss Knell both conscious and a little better. At 11:00 a.m., to my great joy and relief, Mr Holder walked into the courtyard.

During the night, he told me, God had awakened him and told him to get the first train to Niliang, as we were in trouble. Later that day we were able to take Miss Knell by stretcher to the station and so by train to Kunming, where she was safely settled in the hospital.

Some few weeks later while we were having lunch, Dr Chang joined us in a very distressed state of mind. Early in the morning, he said, the entire student body from Kunming, girls as well as boys, had passed through Niliang on their way to join the approaching Communist armies from the south. Among them was his eldest daughter, a middle school student and a lovely Christian girl. Without any hesitation he hurried after them, and after what seemed an interminably long walk he reached his daughter, but to his great consternation she would neither listen to him nor return home. She was a completely changed person, he said, hard and indifferent to the suffering she was causing her parents.

At length he had to make the long journey back alone after seeing his gently-bred daughter shoulder her *pu-kai,* (mattress) and cooking utensils and march off with the rest without so much as a backward look.

We never did hear of her returning to her home and loved ones, but prayed continually for God's watchful care to be round about her.

It seemed, however, that in the days that followed, Dr Chang's shoulders became more bowed and his face lined with sorrow. He was a broken man.

Time went on. We had returned to Niliang, and away from the capital, we continued to live a fairly peaceful existence. With no radio or newspaper we were unable to follow the political developments and there was no noticeable change of attitude of the people towards us. They greeted us kindly, treated us courteously and mentioned little of the changing events. We learned the news from various visitors who passed through, but on the whole life seemed to be quite normal.

We were seriously disturbed therefore one evening when two American AOG missionaries, the Misses Hildebrand, twin sisters whom we knew very well, arrived looking dishevelled in appearance and shocked almost beyond speech. We gathered their story from the Chinese evangelist who accompanied them.

They were on their way to Kunming when the truck in which they were travelling was stopped by Communist brigands and the passengers made to alight. They were then divided into three groups, the third group consisting of the two sisters, who were incidentally the only white people among the passengers. Their evangelist begged to identify himself with them and this was granted.

It was a depressing day, pouring with rain and the place offered no shelter whatsoever, just a few boulders in an otherwise barren spot.

One woman with a young baby, whose husband

had defected from the Communist armies, were shot there and then, their bodies left lying where they fell. Then the brigands, mainly young men, went aside to discuss what they should do with the foreign devils for, having witnessed the shooting, it was imperative that their mouths be shut also. The evangelist at great risk crept up behind a boulder to listen to their conversation, and to his dismay, heard them planning to kill the two missionaries. After creeping back to the sisters he knelt with them in the pouring rain and together they prayed for God to deliver them.

They were rudely interrupted by the brigands who roughly snatched off their wristwatches and other jewellery, took their handbags, helped themselves to the contents and told them they were to be shot. The brigands didn't all agree, however, on this decision. One of their number particularly objected to such drastic measures and there was much arguing and shouting among them, almost coming to blows, but finally they agreed to let them proceed on their journey, forbidding them to ever come that way again.

Just when they were ready to move off in the truck, the young brigand who had intervened and indirectly saved their lives, whispered to them that he had once attended a Mission Sunday School. How wonderful.

We lavished our care upon them and then gratefully knelt to give God thanks for His tender watchful care.

Later on in the evening as we were standing at the door of the Gospel Hall seeing the folk off home after the service, three men walked briskly down the centre of the street. I saw Thelma Hildebrand's face blanch as she looked at them. They were some of the brigands who had so cruelly treated them that very afternoon.

Fortunately they didn't see us, and the next morning the sisters left by train for Kunming. Within a few days they flew home to the United States. I never saw them again. Their lovely little home in Luliang, south of Niliang, with its many treasures, many as gifts gathered over the years, was lost to them for ever.

For several months, one of the twins was so desperately ill that the doctors despaired of her ever recovering. Eventually they settled to live quietly in one of the flats provided for missionaries in Springfield, still bearing the marks of their suffering, but without any bitterness in their spirits.

As they have suffered, so they shall reign.

Not long after this episode, I was approached by the young resident doctor of the newly opened hospital in Niliang to see if I would do the obstetrics there. I could carry on with my evangelistic work, he said, and in the event of the imposition of Communism, would be well protected. This appealed to me.

I didn't want to leave China and knew Miss Knell intended to stay too, so with Government forms which had to be signed by a senior missionary granting me permission to stay, I travelled up to Kunming.

Arriving at *Lu-Shui-Hu,* I found some of the

missionaries already selling their belongings in preparation for leaving. Two days later we had a farewell evening for our American friends, who were flying out en bloc next day.

News was grim. Rumours that our only escape route by air was to be shortly closed did not help to ease the tension. Our Overseas Mission Council had written suggesting that we seek God for guidance individually. And as they were totally unable to meet the financial requirements of flying us all out, we were to sell what we could, to see us safely to our next field of appointment.

As I had elected to stay, however, this didn't concern me, or so I thought — until one revealing incident, which occurred when a Chinese middle school teacher made a most improper suggestion and indeed meant it very seriously.

So it was made clear to me and to other missionary personnel, how impossible it would be for a single woman to stay on alone. I therefore returned to Niliang, packed all my things and joined the other missionaries at *Lu-Shui-Hu* in one of the most humiliating experiences I have ever known, that of selling our belongings.

In Hebrews 10:34 the church is commended: *"when all you owned was taken from you, you accepted it with joy."*

I believe there is special grace given to do just that, but as I saw my beautiful embroidered tablecloths, bed linen and towels, lovingly gathered over the years, the antique crockery, fine bone china and beautiful ornaments, many of them given at great sacrifice by friends and loved ones, treasures and relics of nursing days, roughly handled by filthy hands and thrown down with a derisive laugh, I think the grace of God was abundantly multiplied, enabling me to smile and speak to them at all.

We were the butt of many a jibe and sneer in the days that followed. The atmosphere on the streets was unpleasant and there was a pronounced hostility. Even our Chinese Christian friends urged us to go. To linger would endanger their lives.

Most of us had enough money now for air tickets and some of our number began to move off. Mr Parry had already flown out to Rangoon in Burma. Misses Hewitt, Brown and I were flying out the next day to Rangoon also, where Mr Parry was arranging accommodation for us.

What a tearful farewell. Sun-da-ma, the dear old lady who had served the missionaries faithfully for years, couldn't believe that we were actually leaving. As a little token of our gratitude for her services and at her own request, we had bought her a coffin, which now held pride of place in her little room and which we knew would give her a lot of comfort.

The next day dawned bright and clear, with one of those brilliant skies, only seen in China. The hills stood starkly clear, like sentinels guarding this ancient city.

Never had Kunming seemed such a desirable place, or the people so dear as we sadly made our way to the airfield. It was hard to believe that we were leaving China, probably for ever.

Mr and Mrs Wood, who planned to fly out to Hong Kong during the next few days, together with Mr and Mrs Colley and the Butchers, who had just arrived in Kunming from up country, accompanied us as well as quite a number of Chinese friends.

We were all too sad for conversation, and as the plane rose into the air, we waved through a haze of tears. Lost in thought, we looked down with nostalgia on the familiar landmarks as we flew over the great lake and the paddy fields of the plains, with the hundreds of little villages dotted all over. Would we ever see them again?

I thought of the sad farewell with the lepers some weeks before, and all the many young friends I had loved among the Chinese. I thought of Miss Knell in Niliang and Miss Graves in Milo. What would happen to them, two brave single women facing alone the incoming Communist armies and the inevitable upheaval of the takeover?

Then there was our uncertain future. Misses Brown and Hewitt were hoping to join Mr and Mrs Livesey, our missionaries in Madras, India. Some were making for Bangkok and others were on their way to Japan.

During the last few days and weeks, in spite of the pressures, we had sought definite counsel and guidance of the Lord, but it was undoubtedly one tentative step after another and the future seemed so uncertain.

I felt a leading to pursue my original call to the Tibetans, perhaps now from the India side, and was therefore making for Calcutta, to the address of the American AOG headquarters, where I trusted God would reveal the next step.

How weak and faltering is our faith! We tremble because of the unrevealed future and long to see the whole way, but God invites our implicit trust and obedience. He has delightful surprises ahead if we dare to trust Him.

For the Christian who is daily led by the Good Shepherd, there is a sure and certain plan, *"He calls his own sheep by name ... he walks ahead of them, and they follow him because they know his voice."* (John 10: 3,4) Every situation is a tried way, prepared by One who has already gone before.

In my wildest dreams I could not have imagined such a perfect solution to my problem as that which God in His tender love and care was planning for me.

Idris

10

A New Life

We arrived in Rangoon in the early afternoon and were met by Idris Parry, who guided us through the various formalities and saw us safely to the YWCA, where he had arranged accommodation.

Burma was in the throes of civil war.

The Communists were pressing from the north and had already occupied one section of the city of Rangoon. We were introduced rather precipitately into this situation one evening, a few days after our arrival, when a Chinese friend taking us to a meal, accidentally drove behind the Communist lines.

There were a few ugly moments while our true identity was being checked, the Communist soldiers insisting we were spies, but after a silent lifting of our hearts to God, we produced enough evidence to convince them we were innocent missionaries in transit. They finally let us go with a caution.

The city of Rangoon was beautiful, with its lush foliage and brilliant flowering trees and shrubs; perhaps one of the most colourful spots in the Far East. The streets, with their thronging crowds of people, were a kaleidoscope of colour. It was a cosmopolitan population.

The Indian ladies in their pretty saris, mingling with the lovely floral gowns of the Chinese and the carefree Burmese women in their colourful sarongs, gay scarves and jewellery, lent gaiety and brightness to an already colourful scene.

Dominating the city and towering 300 ft above the heads of the people was the famous golden pagoda, glistening in the sun, as the rays caught the gold leaf with which it was covered.

Hundreds of pilgrims could be seen ascending and descending the steps to the many temples and shrines of the gods. Richly-clad women mingled with the poorer peasant class; the saffron robed monk with his clean-shaven head rubbing shoulders with the American tourist.

Together with a Burmese friend, I climbed the hundreds of wet, muddy steps, only to be turned away by an irate priest, backed by a number of angry pilgrims who objected to the wearing of ankle socks.

We were privileged to see something of the tremendous work that Adoniram Judson began, when as a young missionary aged 25, he sailed for Burma and through years of hardship, privation and persecution, bravely pioneered the Gospel.

It was here in Rangoon that I took my first 'walk' with Idris Parry, a notable event indeed. I think he knew that I guessed his invitation to join him in visiting the famous zoo was simply an opportunity to get to know each other.

We found great joy in one another's company and a bond was forged that afternoon which strengthened with every passing day, until it finally culminated in a marriage which has stood the test of time.

On October 11th, we three ladies, together with the two gentlemen, Idris and Father Morse, an Episcopalian brother, also from China, embarked for Calcutta. It was a small ship and a stormy voyage; consequently we spent three turbulent days of seasickness before finally sailing into the calm waters of the Hoogly River, and so into the great port of Calcutta.

The night was dark. A fierce wind howled around the dock yard and buildings. The rain lashed down, making the Customs shed with its ceaseless human traffic filthy beyond description. Feeling completely drained of life, after the harrowing experience of the past few days in the Indian Ocean, I must confess we looked at Calcutta and its people through jaundiced eyes, especially when the Customs Officer insisted on opening all our cases and was not too careful when handling the contents.

Once again we were strangers in a strange land, not understanding a word of the language and wondering where we were going. One comforting thought was that Idris was also making for the same address as me, so I was not alone in this frightening new situation — another of those wonderful divine arrangements.

Having seen the two ladies safely into a ghari, (horse carriage) on their way to the YWCA, and Father Morse to join his own particular brotherhood, we made our way to Tiljala Road.

"I was a stranger and you invited me in" (Matt 25:35) might well be applied to the American friends who opened their hearts and home to us, showering us with kindness. We can never forget their lavish generosity, the warmth of their friendship and hospitality, which made life very wonderful for us in the days that followed.

As for Idris and myself, our love for each other was growing apace and we felt the blessing of the Lord upon it, so that within a few days of our arrival in Calcutta we became engaged and, subject to the approval of our Home Board, decided to get married as early as possible.

How to finance such a wedding never entered our heads. We had no money whatsoever; but we were assured that this was God's will for us and therefore knew that every need would be met.

In the meantime disaster struck again when I was taken very ill with what was at that time an incurable tropical disease. Suffering intense pain, with my right foot and leg highly inflamed and swollen and with a raging fever, I was taken into a nursing home late in the evening of October 21st. I remember nothing much of those first two or three days; blinding headaches kept me prostrated in a darkened room, while my leg and foot throbbed with pain. I only knew that Idris was now filling the role of father, mother and everyone else combined, fetching and carrying and visiting most of the day. Fortunately we had got engaged the first day of my illness, so we were in the clear with the nationals.

The malaria was quickly brought under control but the leg, which looked to me like an angry cellulitis, had now been diagnosed as filaria with a symptom being elephantiasis. This is a disease introduced by the mosquito which attacks and destroys the lymphatics, progressing with every new infection until the patient becomes a hopeless cripple. The parent worms, in the event of an attack, breed rapidly, but never die themselves, hence the incurable nature of the disease.

A new and expensive drug, Hetrazon, had been produced in the United States, and this eventually destroyed the infant worms, causing the inflammation to subside, but the outlook apart from God looked hopeless.

Letters began to arrive from home. One veteran ex-missionary advised me not to get married, whilst another experienced missionary urged me to return home.

It was the end of my career; depressing words had we not known a Mighty God, but what are a few worms to Him who created all things. The biggest shock, however, was to learn the extent of our debt to the doctor and nursing home; truly in India it was cheaper to die!

Although we pooled our resources, we could not meet the bill, and I was obliged to take my own discharge and return to Tiljala Road with an urgent SOS to our Overseas Mission Council for help.

Fortunately I was now responding to treatment, but had to report for blood tests at the Pathological Department every ten days. The charge for this, expensive at the time was 15 shillings. The result each time ... still thousands of germs in my bloodstream. I made a tentative visit to the Tropical Diseases Hospital where treatment for filaria was free. But the caste-system spotlighted me as a white mem-sahib without shame, and I was obliged to leave.

So I was cast back on God. He who delights in doing the impossible, makes our extremities His opportunities. Mrs Troak, the Elim Minister's wife, who had been greatly used in the healing of the sick, arranged a meeting in her home, where special prayer was made for my recovery.

Praise the Lord: the power of God was present to heal; and from that moment I can testify to a complete and perfect deliverance. Some years later, while home on furlough I was examined by Dr Cook, a Harley Street specialist, who pronounced me free from any filarial worm.

God had done a perfect work — praise His Name.

We had now received the OK from our Home Board regarding our forthcoming marriage, and the date was fixed for December 17th. What a challenge.

Following our marriage we were to proceed to the Indian/Tibetan border, where Mr and Mrs F. Winward had already started work among the Tibetans, and where Mr and Mrs R. Colley from China had now joined them. This meant of course the need to set up home again, as well as the formidable expense of the wedding.

What a glorious thing to be in such a situation, where one is able to stand and see God working it all out beautifully. I cannot remember harbouring any undue worry, though I suppose we did have our moments. Perhaps the relief of sharing our cares and concerns with one another lessened the load; there was no cloud in our sky.

We had enjoyed wonderful fellowship with an American family who lived in the bottom flat of Tiljala Road, Mr and Mrs D. Morocco and their three lovely boys. Mrs Morocco was now expecting her fourth baby and looking forward to a little girl joining the family. To save her the expense of a doctor and nursing home fees, I delivered her in their home, where she was able to have her husband by her side.

Notwithstanding the little disappointment of yet another boy, they were so grateful for the safe delivery and nursing care that they decided to finance the wedding. Mrs Morocco ably stood in for my mother and shouldered all the responsibility.

This was God's marvellous provision for us, and the gesture appealed tremendously to the rest of the American AOG missionaries, who together planned a superb wedding in which Idris and I just played the part of the bride and bridegroom. I will not weary you with the elaborate preparations, but that wedding was all that a girl could ever dream of.

A flower-decked church and rose bower, satin carpet, and a beautiful bridal party complete with a small flower girl who scattered rose petals as I followed her up the aisle.

There was also a crowded church and beautiful service, including an Italian tenor who sang to us as we stood at the altar, followed by a great reception with a hundred guests out on the flower-decked lawn at Tiljala Road, complete with Indian bearers and a magnificent three-tiered cake.

It was all so overwhelming, that it brought tears of joy and gratitude and a heartfelt worship of Him who had so wonderfully planned it all.

That wasn't the end of the kindness of our benefactors, who provided for us to spend a fortnight honeymooning at one of their stations in Purulia before proceeding up to the Tibetan border. We can only say that such kindness will not go unrewarded. *"When you did it to one of the least of these my brothers and sisters, you were doing it to me!"* (Matt 25:40)

With useful wedding gifts from so many friends, we now had sufficient to start up home, and it was with great excitement that we set out on our long trip to Kalimpong.

The train journey took us to Siliguri, the rail head — two days and a night of wearisome travel. We shared a four-berth sleeping compartment with two Indian gentlemen, but there was little rest that night. At every station there was loud knocking on the door of the compartment and angry shouts demanding entry. On one occasion I remember waking up from a fitful sleep to find the compartment full of Indian people. What a major operation it was to get them out again! I was full of admiration for Idris who, without any knowledge of the language, successfully removed them and made doubly sure the door was securely locked.

Arriving in Siliguri we had some difficulty engaging a car and driver to take us up to the hills, but after much wrangling over the price, we eventually started on our way.

How can I describe that breathtaking ride? Once again I marvelled at the luxuriant vegetation of the plain, with its banana groves and tropical fruits, the colourful flowers, plants and shrubs, the exquisite orchids and vivid butterflies, the occasional tribe of monkeys and other wildlife.

Then the tortuous climb up into the mountains and our first glimpse of the mighty Himalayas with their snow-capped peaks. The tree daisies and poinsettias provided a gorgeous dash of colour against the azure blue of the sky.

What magnificent scenery!

The cool air from the mountains fanned our hot cheeks as we climbed ever higher, until we rolled into the quaint little town of Kalimpong.

There was still 1,000 ft to climb before we reached Dr Graham's homes, where we were to share one of the spacious cottages with Mr and Mrs Colley.

As we climbed up through the woods, noisy with the sound of cicadas, we passed the first cottage, Aharva, a missionary guest house. Little did we know that the lady in charge of this home was to be our first contact and a dear friend, who would be the means of opening up a range of wider ministry for Idris.

At various levels among the lovely hills, we saw

one after another of the "homes", each housing thirty to forty children, ranging in ages from little ones of 5 years old to boys and girls of 15 and 16 years of age. Ten or twelve such cottages dotted the hillsides, some occupied by boys, others by girls, each with its own housemother and aunty, and often a teacher too.

There was a farmhouse where a lovely young Scottish couple lived and worked, a school which educated the children up to entry for university, a hospital with its own resident doctor, and a kindergarten catering for the little ones from a few months old to the toddling stage; a community, complete in itself.

In the days which followed, we learned something of the vision that drove Dr Graham, a young Scotsman, to make this great venture in order to cater for the homeless and neglected Anglo-Indian children.

The cottage where we were now to live with Mr and Mrs Colley, "The Scottish", was empty because of lack of funds. We were certainly happy to live in such a spacious house, with its beautiful sur-roundings and ideal climate. A climb of a few feet through the woods at the back of the house, brought us to the peak of the hill where, directly opposite, the great Kanchenjunga range of mount-ains stood.

Although we were lonely at first, the opport-unity for ministry soon presented itself, barriers were broken down, and then we enjoyed marvellous fellowship. Most of the staff from many different countries were evangelical and sound in doctrine, and we made life-long friends.

We were now busy learning Tibetan; but studying together was a tremendous help, and we made rapid progress.

We soon learned of course that living in the "Homes" isolated us from the peoples of Kalimpong, including the Tibetans, but for language study they were ideal surroundings.

Our efficient Nepali boy looked after us like royalty and we felt like royalty during those first early months of our marriage. After some time, however, Mr and Mrs Colley, feeling like ourselves the need to get closer to the Tibetans, found a little flat to rent in the bazaar, leaving us with the full rent of "The Scottish". This precipitated our next move.

The apostle Paul said he knew how to live on almost nothing or with everything: *"I have learned the secret of being content in any and every situation, whether well fed or hungry, whether living in plenty or in want."* (Phil. 4: 12) I suppose we, in a much lesser degree, had learned to do the same.

Our next home, just a mile on the other side of the bazaar, was a tiny square bungalow which fitted snugly into the hillside. They called it our Dove-cote. It was built by an Anglo-Indian as an overflow guest house to a much larger bungalow situated on the plateau at the top of the hill. So tiny and yet compact, the entire place would have fitted easily into one of the spacious rooms of the "Scottish".

The view from the windows, however, amply compensated for the rather cramped quarters and lack of space. We now looked out on the eternal snows, one majestic peak after another, and some of the sunsets were breathtaking in their grandeur.

Kalimpong was a mountain town 6,000 ft above sea level, which gave it an ideal climate and scenery that was a photographer's dream. Its population was cosmopolitan. Mingling together in the bazaar were Lepches, Tibetans, Chinese, Bhutanese, Nepalese, Indians and Sikkimese, as well as quite a sprinkling of British and Americans.

The pukka-sahibs still lived in their beautiful homes dotted here and there on the hillsides, and now, with the Communist takeover of China, there was a considerable influx of people of various nationalities including more missionaries such as from Sweden and Denmark.

It was a hotbed of intrigue. Many magazine articles could be written about some of the characters that had moved there: the Prince of Greece studying phrenology; the Prince of Mongolia, with his American wife, and several notable and wealthy Chinese banished from their homeland, who had now come to reside in Kalimpong. Little wonder that reporters from *Life* and *Time* magazines also found their way to this enthralling and fascinating part of the Tibetan border.

11

The Tibetans

The Tibetans were fascinating people, tough and tall with strong handsome features, a curious mixture of Mongoloid and European, their brown faces wrinkled from the constant exposure to the harsh climatic conditions of those high Tibetan plateaux. Striding into Kalimpong with their mule trains at the end of a long trail, the muleteers made a striking picture in spite of matted hair and clothes which were dirty and smelly, a marvellous breeding ground for lice.

The wealthy Tibetan astride his magnificent beast made a splendid sight. His national dress gave him the appearance of a land buccaneer; jaunty, colourful, strong and proud. It consisted of a tall fur hat, with a red silk cord entwined in his hair and long earrings denoting his rank, and a high-necked silk shirt. He also wore a dark red tunic girded and hitched up at the waist, forming a capacious pocket, accommodating all he required for the journey. Not forgetting the breeches tucked into his colourful, gartered boots, an ornate sword or dagger by his side, prayer beads around his neck and wrists, so necessary on the long journey, all completed a picture which never failed to thrill us.

Watching them as they set out on the return journey some days later was an event which stirred the whole town. The yak wool had been sold and in its place the mules were laden with cases of tea, biscuits, cloth and other commodities. Every preparation had been made for the road.

These were superstitious people and so a mirror fixed on the forehead of the leading mule guarded against a possible encounter with demons on the route, the idea being that if the demon saw itself in the mirror, it would flee.

Bells hanging around the necks of the beasts made merry tinkling sounds as they trotted along and also warned oncoming caravans of their approach. This was essential when negotiating some of the narrow mountain passes, where it often became necessary for one caravan of mules to lie down whilst the train travelling in the opposite direction walked over them.

Yak tails, dyed red, hung from the necks of the mules, while colourful prayer flags, fastened to their pommels, fluttered supplications heavenwards in the morning breeze.

The Tibetans themselves were in great form, shouting to one another as they walked alongside, or singing tuneless little ditties of their own. One or two of them had washed and spruced themselves up. De-lousing had been done at the side of the road; a bowl of water receiving the bugs and lice as they picked them from clothes and hair, so the devout Tibetan satisfied his conscience by not killing with his own hand, what might possibly be one of his ancestors.

The dogs, great powerful beasts — a kind of Chinese chow — accompanied them. They too wore red ruffs around their necks, giving them a circus dog appearance.

With their carefree attitude to life (a characteristic of the Tibetans), a friendly approach and a naive simplicity which had its own appeal, we were soon on a friendly footing with them, though language limitations barred us as yet from venturing too far into conversation.

Ni-ma, our teacher, was a clever young man who had been secretary to the Prime Minister of Tibet until his marriage to a Chinese girl forced him to leave and they settled in Kalimpong. His appearance made it difficult to believe he was Tibetan; always dressed in a smart Western suit with collar and tie, hair neatly cut and groomed, he looked a typical Westerner. His command of English was excellent.

From him we learned much of the religious system (a type of Buddhism), and the mysteries which surround this forbidden land and her people. This included endless cycles of reincarnation; the hot and cold hells, seven of each through which they must pass; and the constant effort of accumulating merit. The zeal and fear of their beliefs was evident in every part of their lives, dominating and directing them from the cradle to the grave.

So it was that the abovementioned beads at the wrists and neck were counted monotonously as they muttered to themselves the sacred Tibetan prayer. "O-mane-padme-hom" (Hail thou jewel in the Lotus). Or they carried prayer wheels — small metal cylinders packed tightly with rolls of calico on which were printed the same prayer. Rotating these on a handle, they believed they were supplicating heaven as they walked along.

Larger metal cylinders encircled the monastery, fixed to its walls by a frame and stamped with the same words, flicked by the priests and pilgrims as they passed by to attain more merit.

The prayer flags were everywhere; fluttering from the eaves of every Tibetan house, surrounding the inns and Lamaseries, and marking the great trade route to Lhasa itself.

How sad is a religion which demands so much praying but is powerless to answer and at the end of a lifetime's devotion, can offer only Nirvana ... nothingness.

We spent many precious study hours telling Ni-ma of the love of God who reconciled a rebellious world to Himself, through the death of His own dear Son Jesus, and we remember the solemnity and sacredness of that moment when the light began to dawn on his soul and we could feel God's Spirit hovering over him.

What a mighty miracle is the new birth that replaces fear with a wonderful liberty, and remakes a man.

With Ni-ma's help, we now began to prepare simple Gospel messages, and after a few months, launched into open-air work. How much those great husky Tibetans understood of our first efforts to preach we didn't know; indeed, we had serious doubts. However, their tremendous sense of humour was one of their lovable traits and they laughed good naturedly at our mistakes. Though we were often frustrated, we could only pray that something of the glorious message we preached was being understood and received.

Later on we used flannelgraphs to illustrate the Bible stories. Like children they loved pictures and stared in fascination as we stuck them on the board, where strangely, most of the time they stayed. Sometimes, however, a sudden gust of wind would whip away every figure, scattering them in all directions. Then the Tibetans would laugh uproariously, chase after them like children, delighted if they could stick them back on the board. Order restored, we would begin again, capturing their attention as the story proceeded, only to have the same thing happen again.

There were at times more serious interruptions, such as the day when one of our listeners spotted a long-time enemy among those whose attention we had gained. Immediately drawing his knife, he would have killed the man on the spot had not his friends held him down until the other made his escape.

At one time, a procession of Hindu zealots, filing past over and over again with much banging of drums and clashing of cymbals, tried to disrupt what we were doing and prevent us preaching the Gospel. We remained undaunted, however, and waited for the day when we would see some of these lovely men and women turn to Christ. We had the privilege of preaching to people who had never heard the Gospel before. What a thrill that was and how simple our presentation of it had to be!

The supreme being, so far as the Buddhist Tibetans were concerned, was the Dalai Lama, who lived in Lhasa, the capital city of Tibet. The very name Lha-Sa meant 'God's place'. It was necessary therefore to use another name in speaking of the God of Heaven and Earth. Gun-Cho helped them to differentiate. We found it necessary not only to be simple, but to repeat over and over again this wonderful message, the simple message of the cross.

Even so, as they listened to the details of the death of Jesus perhaps for the tenth time, they listened with rapt attention. To see those rough men of the mountains, their strong faces so serious, held in the grip of the greatest story ever told, was something we will always cherish.

We had learned by now that if we desired to reach all classes of Tibetan society, it was important, not only to speak the common language (vernacular) but also the honorific and high honorific. This meant of course that sometimes in order to reach each member of our congregation, we had to say the same thing in three different ways. It certainly drove the message home!

One day some Buddhist lamas stopped to listen to our preaching and seemed very interested. They complimented us on the use of their language and said the message was good. Over the ensuing months we developed quite a friendship with one of them who had a definite hunger for spiritual things and would often seek us out to talk over the great things of eternity. We often wondered if he was a secret disciple of the Lord Jesus.

Visiting him one day, we were taken into the sacred precincts of the lamasery itself. When our eyes adjusted to the darkness, lit only by one or two small butter lamps, we saw him among a group of others sitting cross-legged on the floor, surrounded by many garish images, automatically muttering prayers, or chanting doleful dirges.

We felt the darkness of that place and it made us more determined than ever to present the truth of the Gospel of Christ to these precious people.

12

Landslides and Disasters

The monsoon began in early June with incessant torrential rain for three days and three nights. We had known heavy rains in China, but had not seen or heard anything like this. The sky was black with clouds and the unnatural gloom was illuminated by frequent flashes of lightning, while thunder vibrated and reverberated around the mountains. We were completely cut off and house-bound.

In a short time roads were turned into rivers and the hillsides into hundreds of rivulets as the waters cascaded down. The heavens seemed to open upon us. No one ventured out. We felt isolated and alone in our little cottage on the hillside.

The noise was deafening and the complexion of the countryside changed dramatically as the first day passed, then the second. Then on the third morning Prisca, our Nepali girl, didn't arrive as usual at 7:00 a.m. We got up to the same leaden sky and ominous sound of rain drowning every other sound. There was no one in sight; we felt marooned, the countryside drenched. At 8:00 a.m. terrifying things began to happen all around us as the top soil became saturated with water to the depth of several feet, and huge sections of the hillside slipped away. Great trees were uprooted and crashed to the ground; local houses tumbled downhill and the cemetery on the opposite hill was carried away, taking the human remains with it.

Roads leading into Kalimpong were engulfed by the landslides, cutting us off from the outside world, while the mountain road connecting us with Darjeeling was washed away, taking with it the railway that linked us to the plains.

Three-storied concrete houses slipped down the hillside en bloc, the foundations still complete. In Sikkim, a natural lake high up in the mountains burst its banks, sweeping away an entire village, including a young English missionary, who because of his tremendous language ability, had been granted permission to work there. His body was never found.

Down the mountainside thundered the torrents of water, unearthing great boulders in its path and carrying them down to the Tista River below, where they were flung around like pebbles in the mighty floods of water.

I was trying to make toast on the old clay stove that morning when an imperative shout from Idris made me move out of the way quickly, as the top surface of the mountain at the back of our house began to move and with an ominous thud, slid down onto the house. Miraculously, our little cottage stood, but the earth piled up and with the main water pipe now severed, water and mud poured into the rooms, forcing us to get out immediately. Rough stone steps cut out of the side of the mountain were our link with the house above. But these steps were now flooded; a waterfall in fact. How we made our way up, I will never know.

With trees crashing all around us, the rain still sluicing down and in a state of shock, we groped our way one step after another, until, with a tremendous sense of relief, we reached the top.

What desolation! Hundreds killed, thousands rendered homeless, whilst Kalimpong itself was cut off from the rest of the world for weeks, and strict food rationing became a dire necessity.

Coolies were engaged to dig our little house clear, but it was many weeks before things were back to normal and we were able to settle in again.

I personally never knew real peace in that place any more, though for lack of other accommodation we were obliged to continue living there right through the monsoon period. Heavy rain-storms during the night often robbed us of sleep.

A few weeks after this harrowing experience, we travelled down to Calcutta for a couple of weeks break and Idris was promptly booked for a fort-night's campaign at the American AOG church there. Following a fruitful campaign we arranged a special farewell service for the last night of our visit, holding it on the top floor of a block of flats just on the outskirts of Calcutta. The Bengalis were celebrating independence that night and feelings were running high. The Communists, cashing in on the occasion, were holding demonstrations in the nearby park. The crowds were in an ugly mood and the police advised us to avoid going near them. Knowing the uncontrollable temper of these people when aroused, we were glad to reach the flats without any encounter. We were, however, apprehensive about our homeward journey.

After a tremendous meeting where we stood praising and magnifying the Lord, we experienced the queerest sensation of rocking backwards from toe to heel at quite an exaggerated angle. I saw that everyone was doing the same; moreover the electric light was swinging at the same rate. Only then did we realise we were in a severe earthquake tremor. This was not a very healthy situation on the top of a six- or seven-storey building. Just at that moment a young man ran in to tell us that one of the tall tenement buildings nearby had collapsed.

We quickly made our way downstairs; but the quake was over and to our great relief, the demonstration had dispersed too, so that we were able to make our way quietly home. Once again, we had proved God's mighty power to deliver.

That was our first experience of an earthquake. However, we were to witness several more during the years that followed, but I must confess, we never did get accustomed to the bizarre sensation of the ground becoming like jelly under our feet.

The next morning we left by train for Siliguri and home. We shared a sleeping compartment with an Indian couple and their two children. I tell you this not because there was anything unusual about our sharing a compartment or that it should be with Indians, but because of events which transpired on that journey, causing us to almost loathe the family with whom circumstances compelled us to be closeted for two nights and three days.

As we travelled over the plains that first day, we saw the devastation caused by the heavy rains. Fields completely under water and crops ruined. Towards evening the train stopped. We were informed that a bridge ahead had been washed away. Before we could reverse to the previous station where we might have found food, water and other amenities, the bridge we had just crossed also collapsed and we were marooned between stations, with bush land (in other words, jungle) on either side.

Idris and I had sandwiches and tea, thoughtfully provided by Mrs Morocco, which would suffice us until the next morning, but what then? There was a kitchen on the train with sufficient rice for one day's meals, but the train was packed with people who needed food. Before nightfall the electricity was cut, leaving us without fans or lighting.

Trying to compose ourselves for sleep under such circumstances was not easy. The heat was oppressive and we dare not open windows for fear of thieves, wild animals and mosquitoes. We slept uneasily.

As for our fellow-travellers, the man snored, the children were fretful and the woman querulous. Before dawn broke the children used the floor of the carriage as a toilet, filling the place with an obnoxious stench. We were now so thirsty we could cheerfully have drunk the waters of the

Ganges. Someone told us of a village through the bush where we could perhaps get some tea, so Idris set off to fill the flasks, leaving me to the doubtful company of a trainload of anxious, unhappy people. But we certainly appreciated the water, when he eventually returned.

The building of a temporary bridge was under way, but when later on a ballast train went over to test it, the bridge dropped a foot and our hopes were dashed. Towards the end of the second day there was almost a riot among the passengers. Telegrams were sent to the Governors of Bengal and Bihar; tempers were frayed, voices raised, and we, the only Europeans, found it safer to stay where we were and thus avoid trouble.

Even so, we were subjected to many derisive remarks. Hunger and frustration were producing a situation which was explosive. Later on in the day, Idris managed to get us a bowl of rice, but had to creep down the back of the train, under cover of darkness to get it. Had he been seen, I believe some of them would have lynched him. It staved off hunger, however, for a little longer.

The second night passed wearily; sleep was impossible and we longed for the morning. Rumours were rife and all kinds of depressing reports were maliciously passed on to us in an attempt to break our morale. Thank God for His peace, which garrisons our hearts under all circumstances.

At 4:00 p.m. the next day, the train gave a great shudder and started to move. Slowly it advanced toward the bridge. The water lapped either side and flowed over it here and there. The silence was almost painful. Every passenger held his or her breath, but slowly and surely we proceeded across the fateful bridge and safely reached the other side, to the great joy of the people, who shouted and cheered, leaning so far out of the carriages that it seemed they would surely fall into the swirling floods around us.

We spent yet another night on the train, but with lights and fans working and running water, it was no penance, and early the next day, after a good breakfast in Siliguri, we were on our way up to the hills and home.

13

Pioneering the Gospel

We now had the opportunity of moving into a two-roomed flat directly on the Lhasa Road, rented to us by a Nepali who lived with his wife in the room below. The filth was indescribable, but by dint of hard work we made it clean and fit for habitation. Idris, I remember, removed dozens of long nails from the walls; the mystery of their purpose was never solved. We only know that it took hours of work just to pull them out.

Now, however, it was bright with chintz covers, pretty paper curtains and cushions, whilst an elegant brass table, (bought second hand from a retiring missionary) gave the room a rather distinguished look. Trunks were camouflaged and used for seats; no one was any the wiser unless they sat on them for a considerable length of time, when the lack of padding certainly took its toll.

` Our little veranda, gay with geranium plants, looked onto the Lhasa Road, the main trade route to and from Tibet. We were extremely happy there; the fear of landslides was gone.

The Tibetans were all around us, living underneath and passing along the road continually. The monastery was just on the hill at the back, and we were often awakened to the distant tinkling sound of the mule trains as they approached Kalimpong. All through the season the caravans came and went. We simply leaned over the balcony and chatted to the Tibetans at our leisure, getting to know many of them personally. When the opportunity arose, we rented an empty shop next door, using it for preaching and selling Gospel literature. With many beautiful illustrated posters on the walls portraying the varied Bible stories, it was not difficult to entice the Tibetans in. They loved a story and to see that room full of these lovable, tousle-headed, sometimes dirty, often smelly folk of the mountains gazing wide-eyed at the pictures and asking numerous questions was an opportunity which we grasped with both hands.

How many of them really came through to salvation it would be hard to say; our congregation differed every day. One evening however, as we were taking a little walk on the mountain path at the back of our house, we met a party of Tibetans heavily laden with packs, starting out on the long trail home. Their faces lit up as they saw us, and rummaging in commodious folds of their gowns, they produced Gospels and other literature, telling us eagerly that during the past few days they had heard us preach about Jesus and had simply believed in Him. Now they were going back to tell their families the good news. So we had to leave it, having sown the seed liberally, leaving the results to the great Lord of the harvest.

There was an auspicious occasion when the bones of a notable lama were carried with great pomp and ceremony to the monastery on the hill. All the Tibetans — men, women and children — dressed in their finery for this occasion, their beautiful high-necked silk shirts and blouses, fur trimmed hats and figured boots, with the multi-coloured aprons for the women, presented an array of colour and magnificence that all photographers, amateur and otherwise sought to capture.

The lamas, in full regalia, made a splendid sight as they led the procession carrying ornate incense burners, followed by the band, trumpets of various sizes, drums and cymbals. Some of the trumpets were 15 ft in length and had to be carried by four men. The sound was weird and dismal in the extreme, echoing around the mountains again and again; and when accompanied by the chanting of the priests it made the spine tingle.

The bones were carried in a golden casket, placed on a red silk cushion and protected by a special multi-coloured silk awning. Winding up the mountainside paths with the backdrop of new colourful prayer flags fastened to thin bamboo poles and stuck in the ground, it provided a magnificent spectacle.

In time we got used to the booming of the 7 ft and 15 ft long trumpets, and they ceased to startle us, but one sound we never became accustomed to was the blowing of the conch shell. Around 3 a.m. every morning we were awakened by this eerie and intimidating sound, starting in the distance and getting nearer and louder until with a terrifying blast that nearly frightened us out of bed, it was blown right outside our door. They told us it was the lamas scaring away the devils. Whoever it was, they must have been told of our reaction, for it ceased, and though our sleep was disturbed regularly at 3 a.m., we were spared the blast immediately outside the door.

One memorable morning a young Scotsman, George Patterson, arrived in Kalimpong after making an epic journey into India from the Hidden Valley of Po, a mountain retreat of the great Tibetan feudal lord, Panda Dopgjay.

George, with his companions, had travelled across high mountain passes of 15,000-16,000 ft, a hazardous journey in which they had endured unbelievable hardship and where even his experienced Tibetan companions suffered snow blindness. His missionary friend, Geoff Bull, had remained behind while George made his journey to India to buy medical supplies and enlist further personnel, chiefly nurses.

What an amazing story he had to tell. Mainly through the treatment and subsequent recovery of a sick child, Panda Dopgjay had extended an invitation for missionaries to accompany him into the great vastnesses of Tibet itself. Moreover, for every hospital opened, they were granted permission to erect a Gospel Hall. This was tremendous news! Those of us who had had Tibet laid on our hearts for years, who had thought, prayed and worked for this moment, were thrilled at such a development and gladly agreed to return with Mr Patterson when all arrangements had been finalised. We had

learned in doing a little medical work and midwifery, of the dire need for nurse midwives. The
Tibetan expression for pregnancy, they told us, was
"one foot in the grave", so called because of the
high maternal mortality rate. But we were confident that, with good antenatal care and expert
help in the actual delivery, the outlook for both
mother and baby could really be significantly
improved.

We had already been invited by a number of
influential Tibetans as well as traders to accompany
them to their land and with an outsize need such
as this the open door was all we waited for. The
opportunity was now within our grasp.

Thrilled, we utilised every possible moment to
learn more of the language in preparation for the
great day. The bazaar work and the beggar
encampment kept us feverishly preparing Gospel
messages, while our little hall underneath the flat
was constantly in use for personal work and
enquiries. We spoke little else but Tibetan those
days and found, to our great delight, a fluency we
had never dreamed of.

An unexpected pleasure was an invitation to
accompany some American friends into the closed
land of Sikkim, to Gantok the capital, where the
Tibetans were holding celebrations. Passes were
obtained with little difficulty.

The journey by car took several hours through
magnificent countryside, down through the hot,
humid Tista valley with its swift-flowing river
running alongside and its woods fragrant with a
varied assortment of flowering bushes and plants.
We saw vivid butterflies darting here and there,

of which we learned there were 5,000 varieties in that area alone. How lovely it all was: rhododendrons ablaze with colour, bougainvillaea of all shades and a vast variety of wild orchids, incredibly profuse as daisies in an English meadow. We longed to linger in such beauty, but the journey took us practically the whole day, and we were eager to reach our destination before darkness fell.

The climb up into the mountains was awe inspiring, as one after another of those great majestic peaks unfolded before our eyes, until, as we entered Gantok, it seemed that only a small valley separated us from the mighty Mount Everest itself.

Little wonder that we were led into a spontaneous worship of Him who created such grandeur.

All we wanted next, however, was that refreshing "cuppa" and bed. We were drunk with beauty and didn't feel we could assimilate any more that day.

The only missionary in this tiny buffer state of Sikkim, high in the Himalayas, was an elderly Scotswoman, right there in Gantok, in charge of a school, and we were quickly directed to her place.

Accommodation was scarce; every available room taken by other visitors. We had brought our own camping equipment, however, and showing us an empty schoolroom, our hostess invited us to make ourselves at home. The next day we were up early, exploring in and around Gantok before the celebrations were due to begin.

The place was humming with life; Tibetans,

Bhutanese and Sikkimese were dressed in their finest silks and jewellery. They looked superb.

The scenery was utterly beautiful, the mighty Himalayan mountains glistening against the vivid blue of the sky, forming a wonderful backdrop to the plateau ringed with prayer flags, where the crowd were already gathering and where the devil dancing was due to begin.

As guests of the Maharajah, we were allotted a place along with other Europeans, near his own tent and therefore had a splendid view. His armed bodyguards, about six soldiers, stood to attention nearby.

The orchestra, seated on a veranda at the front of the monastery, were now tuning up, their 15 ft long trumpets, drums and cymbals producing their weird, eerie sounds that filled the air and echoed around the mountains, a fitting accompaniment to the dancing that had now begun.

For two days we watched fascinated as Tibetan lamas, wearing richly-embroidered costumes, enacted in dance and mime the history of Tibet, the age-old confrontation between the black-hat lamas representing the demon powers of darkness and the red-hat lamas representing the philosophical outlook of Buddhism.

Probably the most grotesque figure was the "King of Hell", fearsome and threatening with his headgear of tiny human skulls. We were happy to see him ride away on a magnificent black charger towards the end of the proceedings.

The celebrations were brought to a dramatic climax with the burning of a huge scroll depicting all their evil deeds. As the leaping flames rose to devour it, the excitement was tremendous, the dancers gyrating with joy as they saw their sins go up in flames for another year.

How we longed to tell them that by simply believing in the Lord Jesus Christ, their sins could be eradicated for ever.

Several wonderful, happy months followed, packed with activity and opportunity, and a rewarding ministry also among the Anglo-Indian young people of the Dr Graham's Homes. George Patterson was still in Kalimpong making valuable contacts and was looking forward to joining his colleague Geoff Bull in the near future. But now, there were disturbing little rumours of Chinese aggression and their possible advance into Tibet itself.

The muleteers were still bringing their wool out to India to sell, but war clouds were gathering on the horizon. Our own field council too were in a state of indecision. It had been decided in our General Conference at home that only a token force of missionaries were to remain on the Tibetan border. Ourselves and Mr T.C. Cross were to return home. This was very upsetting for us all, and in the final outcome, only Idris and I remained, buying up every opportunity of speaking for the Lord, sending as much Gospel literature as we could into Tibet before the already diminishing mule-trains ceased altogether.

14

Lucknow

A happy interlude was a visit to Lucknow down on
the plains. The American AOG missionaries
invited us to their Annual Field Conference and we
enjoyed wonderful days of fellowship, highlighted by
Spirit-filled meetings and gifted ministry. The
rare comfort and luxury of a former Maharajah's
house where we stayed with our host and hostess,
Brother and Sister Barrack, we have never forgotten. It was a massive place compared with our
little two-roomed flat in Kalimpong: large airy
rooms, each with its own bathroom, dressing room,
shower and other luxuries.

Outside were lawns and gardens with an
abundance of flowers; sweet-peas and roses
mingling with the more exotic hibiscus and
bougainvillaea, filling the air with their lovely
fragrance. Sunshine filtered through the trees,
dappling the lawn with its strange designs, all so

very beautiful.

Later on, of course, we found that same sunshine overpowering as we lay on our beds for the necessary after-lunch siesta, drenched in perspiration. Even the fans did little to alleviate the blistering heat that enveloped us as they whirred above us. The only thing that moved was a lizard flicking its tongue out to catch the unwary mosquito.

Perhaps then we thought with nostalgia of the more bracing climate of our hill town, and longed for the cool breezes that blew off the snow mountains.

During the conference days we held a very successful fortnight's evangelistic campaign where we saw God working with us in signs and wonders and gifts of the Holy Spirit. The baptismal service held on the banks of the River Ganges proved to be a glorious climax, as old and young, Indians and Anglo-Indians publicly declared their faith in the Lord Jesus and were baptised.

Driving down to the river in the late afternoon, our host stopped to show us the Monkey Bridge — so named because of the hundreds of monkeys which congregated there. So aggressive and offensive were they that we were almost afraid to go near them. Sacrosanct in their exalted state as "gods", they were allowed free scope to do as they willed, so that they walked the main streets, ran along the awnings of the shops, went into houses and hospitals, stole food from the patients' lockers and helped themselves to the products from the baskets carried on the heads of the women to market.

A Christian lady told us of a humorous incident concerning her daughter who owned a beauty salon. Returning from answering the phone one day she found a cheeky languar monkey intently powdering his nose in front of the mirror. She was not convinced that it improved his looks.

Mrs Barrack, our hostess, told of another incident. Awakening from sleep one afternoon she found the imprint as of someone having been sitting on the bed while she slept, and to her horror discovered a large monkey hiding behind the toilet door. The languars are tall, black-faced, long-tailed monkeys who usually lope along on their hind legs, very much like a man in appearance. They are terrible thieves and will even steal babies if possible.

I remembered how we had seen some of these languars during our honeymoon in Purulia. On Christmas Day, we were having a meal with the orphans out in the grounds, when we noticed several of the languars, sitting on a low wall surrounding the orphanage, intently watching the children. We thought maybe they were waiting to steal someone's dinner. When we enquired of the Chowkidar, (Care-taker) as to their intentions, we were horrified to learn they were waiting for an opportunity to snatch one of the little ones away.

Another nuisance was the sacred Brahmin cow. Often painted gaudily and bedecked with flowers, they could be seen meandering slowly and aimlessly through the busy streets of the city holding up the traffic, or else moving from stall to stall eating the shopkeepers' products without any remonstrance on the part of the owner, though it must be admitted, with some dismay. How sad that the so-called "gods" of India are some of their greatest destroyers.

Poor benighted India, bogged down with its many gods and goddesses, doctrines and cults, its people enslaved by fear and ritualism, all so essentially a part of the warp and woof of their living. We observed this in Kalimpong when we saw our landlord, in the early morning, pouring out his worship to the earth gods, or when travelling by train over the limitless plains, a solitary figure could be seen in the rice fields, kneeling towards the rising sun.

Once we shared a compartment on a train with a Buddhist priest, who sat impassively on his saffron cushion in deep meditation, like the god he worshipped. The Hindu could be seen flicking his beads as he monotonously muttered, "ram, ram, ram" and another sad sight was the devotee making his long pilgrimage to Lhasa by measuring his length on the ground, rising and again stretching himself on the earth.

In India there were so many gods, so much utter and complete devotion, but a darkness that could be felt. Not in the wildest flights of the imagination could one think of the filthy, turbid Ganges River as holy. Yet as we began our baptismal service in the cool of the late afternoon, the pilgrims on the opposite shore were bringing their offerings to the temple and descending the steps into the river where they believed their sins could be washed away. On our side there was much activity. Naked youngsters frolicked on the edge of the water while their mothers bathed. The dhobis did the Mem-Sahibs' washing, beating the garments on the stones, then laying them out in the sun to dry, until the foreshore took on the appearance of a patchwork quilt.

In the midst of all this, two stately elephants with their young came down to the river also, picking their way carefully through the washing without touching any of it — a feat indeed. Then with the mahouts still astride their backs, entered the river and slowly sank beneath its surface with scarcely a ripple to denote where they were. We wondered about the attendants who went under with them, but they must have enjoyed the cooling off process too, for it was repeated several times.

In spite of these and many other attractions, we had a nice little crowd who quietly listened to the old sweet, soul-saving story of the cross, and once again we committed the results to the Lord who gives the harvest.

The winding up of the Tibetan border field was swift and irrevocable. Our hopes of an entry into Tibet itself were now shattered. The Chinese had invaded Tibet; the Dalai Lama had been obliged to seek refuge in India, whilst his mother and other high officials were staying in Kalimpong. The mule trains had diminished considerably and still there were several winter months when the Tibetan passes were not negotiable. We ourselves were due for furlough, with no hope of replacements from the homeland. Added to this, we were now expecting our first child and had been advised by the Scots mission doctor in Kalimpong to get home to England if possible for the delivery.

Once again, it was goodbye to so many dear and wonderful friends. Our hearts were saddened and not a little rebellious at the calamitous situation that was forcing us to make such a decision. All kinds of questions filled our minds, giving us no peace. So near to fulfilling our life's calling and ambition, with tremendous possibilities; barriers breaking down; the door to the forbidden land just beginning to open; and now it was all to end. It is in such moments that we must learn to trust. **His** is the hand that still guides unerringly, however dark and desolate the circumstances may be. **His** all-wise dealings can never be faulted. Yet there are situations that do not have an answer down here.

Our stuff was soon disposed of; the paltry bits of furniture and household goods went to some of our Nepali and Tibetan neighbours while our own personal effects just about filled one decent-size trunk.

We were ready to leave. We had acquainted our American friends in Calcutta of our plans for returning home and were looking forward to spending a few days with them before sailing for England. Imagine our shock, therefore, to find Idris booked and billed for a fortnight's evangelistic campaign! Our remonstrations fell on deaf ears; they laughed as they offered no explanation and we laughed with them as Idris went along with their plans and we were enveloped in the warmth and security of their love once more.

It was practically impossible to get a boat home. Day after day Idris trudged from one shipping agent to another without success. And even the doctor's letter requesting a priority booking did not avail.

God had some pleasant surprises for us, however. In a matter of days, with less than two hours' warning, we were in a chartered plane, flying from Dum-Dum Airport in Calcutta to Heathrow London for the ridiculous sum of £60 each. BOAC were transporting a ship's crew back to England and offered us the two empty seats.

The hurried arrangements made by phone left us with barely one hour to pack, say goodbye to our friends and get to the air offices. We were thrilled at God's marvellous provision for us, and within an hour we were on our way; a taxi taking us to Dum-Dum and the plane which was ready for takeoff.

The flight was not the acme of luxury; there was no air conditioning and in flying over the Alps we were almost frozen to our seats. Wearing the lightest of tropical clothing we were totally unprepared for the temperamental English climate, especially in March; but God lovingly undertook once again and a bright sunny day greeted our arrival.

What excitement I felt as the pilot announced over the intercom that we were now flying over England and we looked down on the beautiful green fields and the hedgerows of the Kent countryside. We shall never forget the joy of that return after so long a time in such different surroundings. "God's own country," one passenger remarked — and we heartily agreed with him as we feasted our eyes on England's green and pleasant land.

The two days spent in London were packed

with activity. Meeting old friends, making essential purchases (I was hatless and stockingless, the latter not acceptable in those days). We had a quick interview with our missionary secretary and enjoyed a ministers' fraternal, where the rich harmonious singing of so many pastors brought tears to my eyes.

It was then on to Preston, home and Mother. Many times in faraway China and on the Tibetan border, in the lonely hours, or when sickness weakened the morale, I had thought and dreamed of this hour; and now it was actually upon us. The train was pulling into Preston's dingy but oh so familiar station. Home at last and my heart echoed the sentiments of one of our Preston girls when she said she loved every "mucky flag" (flagstone). That was a wonderful reunion; the fact that Mother was looking just the same and enjoying good health was such a relief. It was a joy long anticipated: to be welcomed back into the bosom of the family, to sit in front of an open fire, listening to the patter of the rain on the window panes and to talk, talk and talk, about God's goodness and His watchful care while we were absent from each other. Would we ever be able to recount it all? His mighty deliverances and marvellous provision, and the blessings we enjoyed. Like the disciples of old, our hearts burned within us and in like manner too, Jesus Himself drew near. There followed great days of "Welcome Home" services, convention meetings, tremendous missionary rallies and itineraries. We thoroughly enjoyed them all. Not surprisingly one little girl said she would like to be a missionary on furlough!

Our baby David was born on August 26th that same year, 1952; a red-headed, pug-nosed little fellow who won all our hearts. Idris was itinerating in London when the good news reached him. Little wonder that in his dash to reach us, he left his briefcase, complete with sermon notes, on the underground train.

All through the autumn and winter Mother and I enjoyed one another's company. Those were comfortable days. Idris continued his itinerant ministry around the assemblies, coming home for a few brief, treasured hours between one district's meetings and another's. We at home cared for our little one, seeing him develop from a crumpled, red-faced baby to a bonny, curly-headed boy, who filled our lives with joy and sunshine.

The time came, however, for serious contemplation as to where our next sphere of service was to be. We had prayed much about this. The field of our original call was now closed to the Gospel. Did this mean that overseas missionary service was at an end for us, or did a need constitute a call? The AOG Kalembe-lembe field in the Congo (now the Democratic Republic of Congo) was in urgent need of extra personnel and we were approached about this. The Misses Noad and Hegi, two redoubtable ladies, had struggled alone for several years until Mr and Mrs F. Holder, former China missionaries, had joined them about 12 months previously. We learned of the formidable territory, manned only by four missionaries, and the equally challenging vastness of the areas still unevangelised. The compelling strength of the great commission

(Matthew 28: 19-20) sealed our call once again and we offered ourselves for the Congo. This meant, of course, a period of time in Belgium, for study of the French language. And it also meant leaving our son David behind. He was now at the crawling stage, progressing well. It was not easy to leave him for three months with friends, who, bless them, readily took him into their family circle. Neither they nor we, however, will forget the anguish of the exchange afterwards, or our painful experience of finding that David had adopted them as his mummy and daddy. The suffering they endured at parting with him was only equalled by our distress at seeing the obvious bewilderment of our little boy.

15

A Chapter of Woes

Captain Beloved, battle wounds were Thine,
Let me not wonder if some hurt be mine,
Rather oh Lord, let this my wonder be
That I may share a battle wound with Thee.
From fearing when I should aspire,
From faltering when I should climb higher,
From silken self, O Captain, free
Thy soldier who would follow Thee.

Amy Carmichael

We sailed for Africa on the Durban Castle on August 26th, 1953; David's first birthday. The voyage was an unhappy one from the beginning; perhaps a precursor of what was to follow all through the five years of our first term on the Kalembe-lembe field. The badly situated L-shaped cabin, which was to be our home for a month, assumed, for myself at any rate, the miserable confines of a prison. Cribbed, cabined and confined, so aptly describes how we felt from the first day in the Bay of Biscay, until we dropped anchor in Dar-es-Salaam, East Africa. Anyone taking a long sea voyage with an active 12-month-old baby boy in those times would appreciate our position. The heat was oppressive. David seemed to be the unhappiest little mortal on the ship; with fair skin, he suffered the torments of prickly heat which nothing seemed to relieve. Laundry facilities were inadequate, dryers and iron in constant use, so that I found it necessary to wash our underwear and David's nappies in the cabin washbasin. With no circulation of air, however, they became hard and rough, chafing his skin so badly that we were obliged to seek the help of a doctor as soon as we disembarked.

We never solved the problem of how to keep him quiet in the cabin when other passengers were resting. The nights were particularly trying; how does one keep a lusty unhappy baby from crying?

It was a rule on board that children, however young, were to be fed in the dining room before the adults. I came to dread this daily occurrence. Imagine a hot, humid dining room, with children of all ages, anxious mothers, crying babies and toddlers, eating or trying to eat a meal that was quite unpalatable for many of them. It is a memory that will never be erased.

The seas were so rough on occasions that the heaving, rolling and tossing of the ship compelled me to leave David in his high chair, while I dashed to the nearest bathroom. To add further to the discomforts of that voyage, powerful earthquake tremors from the Greek islands affected the sea bed, causing mountainous waves to sweep over the top deck of that great liner. This resulted in such a severe roll that panic was noticeable, especially among the lady passengers, and the Captain had to assure us over the public address system that there was quite a bit of play before we listed to the point of no return. Only the very few good sailors were able to stay around; the rest of us were confined to our bunks, clinging to the stanchions as the ship rolled over at a terrifying angle, lay in that position for what seemed an interminable length of time, then with a tremendous groan, righted herself, only to repeat the same performance in the opposite direction.

For three days we endured this. The thought of food was repugnant. We were told that children were immune to seasickness, but David proved this is not so. He too was very sick, and as a safety measure against the violent movements of the vessel, we moved him from his bunk into mine. Imagine the skill required to keep us both in the bunk in such circumstances. As we rolled to the right, David vomited over me; when we rolled to the left I vomited over him ... Could there be anything more demoralising?

Once a steward popped his head around the door, "Everybody all right in here?" he said. "Can't stop, too many needing attention," and away he went. The third day a Church of Scotland lady missionary with whom we had conversed on several occasions came in, tucked David under her arm, picked up a bucketful of dirty nappies and informed me that she would look after the boy. Oh-h-h ... the relief was tremendous — just to be miserable in peace! And we thanked God for this ministering angel.

Undoubtedly the high spots of the voyage were the frequent ports of call: Gibraltar, Genoa, Port Said, Sudan, Aden and so on as we continued south along the East coast of Africa, spending a day here and a couple of days there while the ship loaded and unloaded freight. These port stops gave us an opportunity to relax, and meant that during this part of the voyage, at the longest we were four days at sea at one time. We were nevertheless very happy to disembark at Dar-es-Salaam and feel terra-firma beneath our feet once more. We found accommodation with a Syrian lady some four or five miles out of the town. The house was already full, as a Swedish missionary family that we had got to know on board ship had just moved in. But as they were expecting to travel on in a day or two, we were temporarily housed in an old barn in the grounds.

It was a corrugated iron structure, crudely erected with plenty of gaps and spaces, allowing air as well as other things to get in; but we were thankful for a resting place. Only those who have had to leave the security of a passenger liner and step onto foreign soil, knowing nothing of their whereabouts and having no acquaintances, can understand the frightening loneliness. We did have a roof over our heads and in spite of its primitive nature, we were glad to compose ourselves for sleep, particularly after the ceaseless movement and noise of the ship. The peace of the compound acted as an opiate and we slept well.

Our proposal of staying there two or three days, however, lengthened into two weeks, as we waited for a booking on the train to Kigoma in Tanzania.

We were not sorry about this delay, as it enabled us to sort ourselves out. We were now occupying a very pleasant room in the house and were on fine terms with our hostess. David too, we noticed, was coming back into his own, his sunny smiles and chuckles replacing the awful lost, bewildered look of the past few weeks. We had occasional picnics down on the beautiful beaches of golden sands dotted with palm trees; secluded little coves between picturesque headlands and the blue sparkling sea which enticed us to swim. However, we found the sun far too fierce for our fair skins and deemed it wise to keep in the shade.

Our hostess had no children, but she did have two little Pekinese dogs. Ticky and Tacky were completely pampered and spoilt. Well fed and beautifully groomed, they dominated the entire household. The ritual each evening was highly amusing, when promptly at 7 p.m. they were carefully and tenderly tucked into their individual little beds, where they lay nestling between the sheets and blankets, their heads on the pillows as cosy as any baby.

Our booking on the train was organised for October 25th. The morning of our departure saw us hurriedly following behind eight or nine men, each carrying one of our trunks on his head as we proceeded to the station. These bearers were noted for their pilfering, so it was essential to keep them all in sight — not an easy task as they quickly and expertly wove their way among the jostling crowds. We made sure, however, that every piece of luggage was intact and safely placed on the train before settling in our own compartment

... what a fallacy. The train had scarcely begun its long, tortuous journey, when the guard appeared and asked us if we would go along and identify our luggage. Where or when the damage was done we never found out. Every lock had been wrenched off and a number of the hinges too, giving easy access to the contents. Fortunately (and to us, amazingly) there was nothing missing; the thief no doubt had been disturbed at the crucial moment, and we were able to secure them with ropes before leaving the train.

We travelled 2nd class to save expense, preparing our own food. But we regretted this decision before the journey ended, as we found it was false economy and healthwise, utterly foolish. The carriage was hot and the simple but necessary commodity of boiled water almost impossible to get. Before we left the train both Idris and I were ill with tummy trouble. The scenery was nondescript, mainly bush country (known as 'jungle' to some) and after two rather boring days of travel, we arrived in Kigoma on Lake Tanganyika.

Here God wonderfully undertook for us. We were feeling ill and completely drained of strength through the constant vomiting and diarrhoea. The dreaded routine of Customs and other formalities; the hiring of bearers; finding accommodation for the night, all seemed so much more of a burden in our state of ill health; but thank God, our weaknesses are known to Him and provided for in His divine economy. So it was that a kind Arab gentleman, seeing our weakened state, helped us with the officials, saw our luggage on to the steamer, which miraculously was in dock and about to sail, and graciously obtained permission from the Captain for us to move into our cabin immediately. God has His angels everywhere. Oh the luxury of lying in our bunks in a pleasant cabin with the cool air blowing in from the Lake! After two days and a night in a stuffy railway carriage with no opportunity of lying down, it was bliss. The day and night's travel over the Lake was quite enjoyable; we had our own little section of the deck to sit and recuperate and we enjoyed the meals, prepared and served by Belgian stewards. The Congo shores were visible for a long time before we finally docked at the port of Kalundu.

At last we had arrived. Our coming had been anticipated for some considerable time by Mr and Mrs Holder, who had worked hard to get the new mission house ready for our arrival. Built on a hill overlooking Lake Tanganyika, it was a lovely place and commanded a fine view. The high windows on the front and side of the main living room had not yet been glassed in, fine wire mesh taking its place temporarily, but otherwise it was complete.

We had been due to arrive the next day and they had been excited at the prospect of seeing us and hearing our news. But they themselves had unexpected news for us ...

They told us that it had been a lovely evening. Tired but exultant, the Holders had lingered on the veranda just before retiring for the night, looking down on the calm stillness of the lake. How peaceful it was, but how unpredictable, as they were soon to find out. They were awakened early the next morning about 4:30 a.m., by the vicious roaring of the wind as it swept up from the lake, battering the house and bending great trees down to the ground in its fury. The noise was deafening; it seemed the very devil himself was on the rampage.

They knew of course that the rainy season was often heralded by unusual heavy storms, preceded also by strong winds, but this was worse than they had ever known and moreover it was increasing in its intensity. They feared for the safety of the house. Suddenly, with an ear-splitting, terrifying sound, the massive tin roof was lifted right off, the force of the wind carrying it over the tall mango tree at the back of the house and dropping it into the bush some little distance away.

Mr and Mrs Holder stood, white-faced and trembling, they told us later, looking at the damage, as vivid flashes of lightning lit up the place. The freak wind, thought to be a tornado from the lake, had swept through the house, scattering everything in all directions. Then the rain came, driving rain that poured through the windows and seeped under the doors, until there was water everywhere, spoiling much of the soft furnishings and playing havoc with books, letters and papers.

The critical moment came when Mr Holder looked up and saw the ceiling boards sagging under the weight of water. Any minute it would collapse around their ears. Picking up a long pointed stick, providentially handy, he quickly pierced every section, allowing the water to sluice through into the room below. Quick action had undoubtedly prevented a further calamity — but what a disaster! In a few hours' time they were planning to leave by car to meet us. What could they do? Before 7 a.m., the local people began to arrive. Bush telegraph is a wonderful thing. Pastors, teachers, workmen and schoolboys stood gazing wonderingly at what had happened. The storm had passed over, but left devastation in its wake: native huts destroyed, trees down and not least, the roof whipped off the new mission house.

The main concern now was to replace the roof before any further storms. Then they remembered the new missionaries were due to arrive, and that was all the spur they needed. Everyone got to work with a will, working all through the day without any break or rest. Before darkness fell, the roof was back in place.

In the meantime we had arrived in Kalundu and wondered why there was no one to meet us. With no knowledge of the local language except for a bit of French, or of our whereabouts, we were in a dilemma. The port was a barren-looking place, just one government building and a few "go-downs", not the sort of place one would choose in which to spend even a short time.

Fortunately some Swedish missionaries, seeing our predicament, promptly took us and our luggage to their mission station in Uvira to await events. Shortly afterwards Miss Noad arrived, looking dishevelled but heartily glad to find us. She told us that Mr Holder had driven over to her station at Nundu earlier in the day, 45 miles along the lakeside from Baraka, and after explaining what had happened, had asked if she could come and meet us. The old Ford truck she had was definitely the worse for wear, but we mercifully didn't know this.

Nor did we know anything of the terrain we must cover on our journey to Baraka.

The native driver seemed a nice enough fellow, Miss Noad had told us his name, but after experiencing a nightmare journey in which he drove like "Jehu", I'm afraid that was the name we gave him ever after.

The night was dark as we started off on the last lap of our journey. Miss Noad, David and I squeezed in the front of the vehicle along with the driver, but Idris unfortunately was obliged to sit in the back, on the floor of the truck, with the luggage packed in around him. This situation might have been tolerable driving on our smooth British roads, but imagine the discomfort of driving over dirt roads with uneven surfaces and numerous potholes, wedged in a narrow space with his back to one side of the truck and feet against the other side.

The driver's only concern was to get back home as soon as possible. Consequently we seemed to fly along the road, bouncing up and down dangerously as we hit one pothole after another, swerving around the corners along the narrow road skirting the lake, and through the villages at breakneck speed.

It seemed we were in the hands of a madman. I trembled to think what might have happened had we encountered another vehicle coming from the opposite direction. But God was good; His angels were not far away.

Miss Noad's remonstrations had no effect whatsoever. Fortunately, squeezed in tightly as we were, we were held fairly steady in the front, although once or twice we almost hit the roof; but I feared to think how Idris was faring in the back. The crunch came when we drove over one of Congo's famous bridges: just tree trunks thrown across a chasm, then two planks of wood laid across the trees. The idea was, that the vehicle should be carefully driven on to the planks and thus over to safety. Our driver, however, without slackening speed one iota, missed the boards and bounced his way from one tree trunk to another.

That was the last straw. Idris had had enough; wedged in he might be, but in desperation he banged on the side of the truck until the sound penetrated above the din and rattle of the engine and we stopped. When he appeared a few minutes later, bruised, shaken and filthy from the dirt and dust of the road, he let rip into that young man, using such a torrent of English that in spite of the language barrier, although the driver didn't understand a word, he nevertheless got the message. Not long afterwards we rolled into Nundu, Miss Noad's station.

It was too dark to see much of the place, but I remember the shock of seeing the primitive nature of the mission house. A low mud and wattle hut with a thatched roof, whitewashed walls and dirt floors, so very similar to the African huts we had seen en route, with the exception that this was bigger. This had been the missionary's home for years. How plucky she was. The lighted lamp threw weird shadows into the corners of the room where we sat drinking a welcome cup of tea, and my mind was filled with all sorts of questions. How could she live in such squalid surroundings? How lonely it must be. Would we have to live like this? What sort of a place had we come to? Thoughts that I dare not put into words lest I be considered "unsuitable". Before we left Nundu, Miss Noad pointed to the silhouette of a brick building nearing completion on the opposite side of the road. "My new house," she announced proudly.

The drive on to Baraka was quite comfortable, with the two of us and David in the front, the young man now not daring to do other than drive carefully. In a little over an hour we passed through Baraka itself, with its one or two native stores and cluster of houses.

The mission house, we were told, was two or three miles further on at a place called Mkuku. Turning at last into the drive that led to our house, our gaze was held by a bright light moving up and down in the density of the undergrowth ahead of us. Could it be fireflies? Or were we so tired that our eyes were not focusing properly? As we drove on, slowly now for the road was narrow and full of holes, the light became brighter and we were able to make out the figures of Frank and Ivy Holder, carrying a storm lantern and coming to meet us.

What a welcome we had! The delight of seeing one another after several years was quite mutual and we chatted merrily around the supper table, all tiredness banished as if by magic. There was still a lot to do in the house after the upheaval of the night, but that didn't seem to matter any longer, and in comparison with Miss Noad's mud hut, this was a palace.

16

First Impressions of Congo

I find it difficult to analyse my feelings of those first early weeks in the Congo. We were not new miss-ionaries by any means and yet, there were now fears we had never known before. Was it perhaps the thought of a bush forest hemming us in, or was it the added responsibility of our little one, I don't know. The latter seems the more probable, but they were real fears. I somehow expected to see a snake under every bush and thought our friends very courageous to wander off through the narrow paths for a little walk after darkness had fallen.

Many times after David had been settled down for the night, the mosquito net tucked safely around him, I would steal into the bedroom with a torch, shining it under the cot and all around the room, just to make sure there were no intruders. I'm glad to say these fears were only temporary, but they were very real at the time.

Two days later, we experienced for ourselves one of the dreaded African storms. Suddenly it seemed, the sky became black with clouds and the air grew chill, while a deathly, almost sinister silence prevailed everywhere. The chirping of the birds and insects had ceased; the only sound to be heard was the muffled voices of the fishermen as they drew their boats to land. When the wind came, it was frightening in its intensity, tearing around the house like some wild thing, flinging loose articles about as though they were matchwood and filling the air with sound. The boughs of smaller trees were snapped off and flung considerable distances away, while the swaying and creaking of the great trees added to the confused noise.

Suddenly, with a high-pitched screaming noise that almost made my heart stop with fright, an extra strong gust tore the corrugated iron roof off the veranda, wrenching out the 5" nails which held it in position and carrying it over the roof of the house, slicing off the top of the tall mango tree on its way.

The driving rain which followed was equally devastating, flooding the rooms in a comparatively short time, so that the men were frantically sweeping water out while Mrs Holder and I endeavoured to rescue valuable papers and letters. The peals of thunder and flashes of lightning were so nerve-racking that I found great difficulty in concentrating on anything, and was very relieved to hear that it wasn't always like this. That same week, the house was shaken by an earthquake tremor. No wonder the local people began to call us

Mr and Mrs Jonah!

Our first Sunday was an unforgettable day. The large church building, holding several hundred, was packed to capacity. Rows of black shining faces, flashing eyes and sparkling white teeth — it was a sight to make the heart glad. There was sheer joy and exuberance in the singing that morning. I had never been so moved. From toddlers, the African children learned to harmonise, and as that wonderful crowd of people lifted their voices in worshipful praise the sound was grand and glorious. We found the special welcome songs particularly moving and it seemed we sat for hours while various groups sang, and clapped or stamped their feet in wonderful rhythm.

After the service, which by our homeland standards was lengthy, stretching on into the afternoon, there was a hand shaking session for us both. Everyone, right down to the smallest boy, insisted on shaking hands with us (a custom introduced by the Belgians). We shook literally hundreds of hands and said, "Jambo", meaning 'hello' and incidentally the only Kiswahili word we knew, over and over again until we felt limp and exhausted.

Later we were introduced to two of our nine very fine pastors, who together oversaw the whole of the work in the vast area of the Kalembe-lembe field. What grand, godly men they were. Men who had hazarded their lives for the sake of the Gospel. We learned to admire and hold them in high esteem. Another two pastors, David and Daniel, together supervised the work in the Baraka area.

Later, at our Christmas convention, we were able to meet all the pastors.

We found the study of the Bantu language, Kiswahili, considerably easier than either Chinese or Tibetan, or perhaps we were getting used to learning languages. This would be our fourth one, including French. There was an alphabet of 26 letters, vowel sounds as in French; and with a pronunciation that was phonetic, we were able to read almost immediately. To sit on the platform in church the first Sunday and be able to sing from the hymn book as though we had been in Congo for years, did something for the morale!

For several years, the Kalembe-lembe field had been without a Bwana (master) at all; now they had two. The mud and wattle buildings which had housed the missionaries for so long were being replaced by more permanent structures. The wind of change was beginning to blow and the local people were delighted. A heavy building programme was still ahead: a new school which we hoped would be subsidised by the Government and at least one more missionary house.

We employed a young boy to care for David during the mornings to enable us to get down to serious study. This proved most difficult, however, and the activities around us didn't help our powers of concentration. Once or twice Idris accompanied Mr Holder on trips to the township to buy building materials, etc., which was so much more exciting than poring over Stear's Swahili handbook. Hauling bricks alone could keep both men fully occupied, but we knew it was essential for us to get a good grasp of the language in order to be of any real use.

As Idris mixed with the local people, however, he found the language opening up to him in an amazing way and he acquired many useful colloquial expressions which we found most helpful and encouraging.

We learned other things too during those early weeks in the Congo, for example, one of our expressions, to be 'jiggered', soon meant more to us than to be 'healthily tired after exertion'.

If we went barefoot, jiggers, (or chigoes) those minute, flea-like insects, almost invisible to the naked eye, but prevalent in the dust and sand of the earth, burrowed their way under our toenails and laid a sac of eggs, the size of a small pea, in the flesh. The process of digging them out afterwards was most painful. It involved carefully scraping the surrounding skin with a needle or sharp knife, exposing and removing the whole of the egg sac, so as to prevent further injections of hundreds of baby jiggers.

I can never forget David's screams as Mrs Holder painstakingly worked on his feet. As a result I personally made sure that he always wore shoes in the hope that he would not suffer this experience again. Some of the local villagers were actually crippled as a result of jiggers, and Mrs Holder treated the more severe cases for an hour or so each morning.

The mango fly was another pest. Emerging at dusk it deposited its eggs on any garment left around. The eggs fortunately could be destroyed with a hot iron, but some of the house boys didn't consider the ironing of nappies necessary at all, or were content to iron just one side of the square, with the result that David had 14 or more mango grubs working under his skin. The angry boil-like eruptions which followed had worried us quite a lot until Miss Noad, our senior missionary, identified them and advised us to wait until they were ripe before squeezing. When we did squeeze them, we were horrified at the size of the fat maggot-like worms which popped out. A few weeks later we were afflicted in the same way. I can only say that the horror of feeling the grub, growing and wriggling in our flesh, was an experience not to be repeated, and we learned a salutary lesson — to make sure all our garments were collected in before dusk.

Preparations were now well ahead for the Christmas Convention. Thousands of Congolese believers were expected to converge on Baraka for this occasion and we looked forward tremendously to it. Large groups would be coming from the plains of Kabambare and the mountains of Lulenge, journeying several days of hard travel on foot, usually barefooted too, bedding and cooking utensils strapped to their backs. Others would be making the trip by water from Lwata and the lakeside villages, the flotilla of canoes making an inspiring sight as they turned into Burton's Bay, taking up formation for the last lap of their journey to the Baraka shore, their rich harmonious voices ringing clear over the water as they sang rhythmically to the dip of the paddles.

To accommodate them was a major operation; the dwelling places of the local Christians being totally inadequate, but where there's a will, there's a way, and miraculously, everyone was squeezed in, whilst the communal sharing of the church was quickly brought into operation. The three days of Convention meetings were wonderfully exciting days of fellowship. The mundane chores of eating and drinking became secondary to the more demanding appetite for spiritual food. Fortunately Mrs Holder and I had had several baking sessions in preparation and the outer man was quickly and easily satisfied. I scarcely remember our own Christmas festivities as the pressure of meetings left us with little time for anything else, though we did have a special Christmas dinner.

The business conference which immediately followed the convention was a unique experience for both Idris and me, although most of the discussions needed to be interpreted for us. We were amazed at the maturity of these Congolese leaders who faced the toughest problems with grace and godliness, and we felt immediately a love that bound us to them. Closer knowledge of them only deepened our admiration as we learned of the sacrifices they had made and their exploits in the furtherance of the Gospel.

17

Sink or Swim

Our baby daughter, Gillian Ruth, was born on 29th March, 1954. An adorable little thing with enormous eyes, she more than fulfilled my expectations, for she was perfect in form and feature and for the first six months, perfect in behaviour too, sleeping from one feed to another in her carry-cot under the thatched veranda of our house in Lulimba. We didn't realise how much of a blessing from God was this quiet well-behaved baby, until we were faced with the terrific demands of a busy station life and the supervision of an area the size of two of our biggest English counties combined, with a still limited knowledge of Kiswahili.

We had waited for baby Gillian's arrival before moving out to man the Lulimba station some 80 miles from Baraka. This included, because of insufficient missionary personnel, the great areas of

Lulenge to the north and Kabambare.

Before our baby was a month old we were on our way. All the schoolboys and teachers lined up that morning to wish us God speed. The old Ford truck in which we had made that eventful journey into Baraka had been placed at our disposal, for it was quite impossible to live in such remote areas without transport. Idris had learned to drive during the past few months and now somewhat diffidently took the wheel, with David and myself in the front with him. Mr and Mrs Holder with the new baby followed in the Chevrolet truck, and we were off to the shouts and waves of a hundred or more school-boys. I think I can truthfully say this was the one and only occasion when I started out for Lulimba with a tranquil heart and mind. I was blissfully unaware of the hazards of that particular route, or the mountain escarpments which in wet weather were perilous to negotiate.

The day, however, was fine; a thrilling new adventure lay ahead and the journey went without a hitch. The escarpment, with its own particular hazards, we hardly noticed.

It was dark before we reached Lulimba. The last two or three miles of our trip seemed to penetrate right into the heart of the bush itself, man-high elephant grass bordering the narrow road that led us to the door of the missionary house. We scrambled down from the truck, glad to stretch our limbs after several hours in a cramped position and eager to take a look at our new house.

In a clearing of several hundred yards, we saw a small mud brick, thatched bungalow. The thatch extended over the walls to form a veranda and was supported by small irregular trunks of trees. The inevitable gap of several inches between the top of the walls and the thatch gave easy access, we learned in time, to numerous unwelcome visitors, including snakes and tree lizards as well as mosquitoes and other unidentified creatures. The front of the house presented a blank wall, broken only by a small door in the middle, the top half of which was mosquito netting. This was to be our home for the next three years.

Trunks and boxes, although not locked, were left outside, some for several days. There was an honesty among the Congolese around us which we saw disappear as troubled times came.

The light from a small lantern was insufficient to enable us to do any serious unpacking, but there were still beds to make up before we could sleep that night. Mr and Mrs Holder had to make the return journey and were anxious to be off, so sitting anywhere we could, we had a cup of tea from the flask, and sandwiches specially brought for this emergency. Then after a word of prayer, they bade us goodbye. I remember we experienced a moment or two of utter desolation as the sound of the car engine faded into the distance, but shaking off the feeling, we got to work, sorting out the various articles needed for immediate use. Our baby was fed and tucked safely under the mosquito net for the night. Miraculously, out of the chaos of boxes and goods, we found David something to eat, fixed up his cot and settled him down. In one of the rooms we found two single iron bedsteads with wire mattresses. These we pushed together and laid our double Dunlopillo mattress on them.

In spite of several inches of wire to spare on both sides, making it difficult to climb in and out, it looked comfortable and inviting. So having tied our mosquito net in position, we decided to call it a day and retired, sleeping until dawn when we were more able to face the chaotic situation.

In the morning the bright sunshine only seemed to accentuate the dismal surroundings in which we found ourselves. The floors were covered with a thick layer of brown dust, blown in by the hot wind peculiar to that area. I remember it continued to blow for several weeks until the sound penetrated our brain, and with so many gaps and openings, a film of dust was deposited everywhere; on beds, food and in our hair.

The house was partitioned off into three small rooms by single mud brick walls. There was no ceiling; empty blackness stretched from the top of the walls to the apex of the thatch. I was so thankful that we didn't have the plague of bats that they had at Baraka. Imagine twenty or thirty of them hanging upside down from this thatch, or flying around above our heads!

Our one pressure lamp, we found, illuminated the whole house. The walls had been recently whitewashed, but already the termites were making inroads in an endeavour to reach the thatch, leaving ugly black grooves in their wake.

A small aperture on the far side of each room, covered with mosquito netting, answered for windows. An opening on either side of the living room led into the two bedrooms. However, the lack of doors was remedied to some extent by hanging curtains to give some degree of privacy. Furniture was negligible.

We anticipated ordering a consignment of wood as soon as possible, seasoning it off and having our own furniture made. But this would take time, so we were grateful for the small wooden table, two upright canvas chairs, a metal cupboard (which we found invaluable) and the two single beds.

The precious missionaries had also given us permission to use their fridge until we could obtain one for ourselves. Let me hasten to add that this house was never intended to be anything other than a temporary dwelling — a more permanent building being envisaged when possible. But in the meantime, we had to make a home out of this barren-looking place and I was thankful for every bit of curtain, a few colourful cushions and the odd bits of brassware and other materials found later in the trunks.

We worked steadily all day, bringing some degree of order out of the chaos. Two of our wooden cases nailed together made an admirable crockery cupboard. Tin trunks, well padded and covered with flowered cretonne, became a settee, whilst another two, covered with plastic, acted as a washstand. A cable case became both bedside table and store for our provisions, and with a cloth on the table, curtains in place and our elegant brass table gracing the middle of the floor, things almost looked normal.

There were countless interruptions of course, a constant stream of people coming and going all day. Some came with real needs, but most of them were curious to see the new missionary family: the blonde baby; David with his red curls;

the fair madam and the dark-haired bwana; to them quite fascinating.

We couldn't attend to their many ailments, as the medicine and tablets were still lying in the trunks, undiscovered as yet. But we had a feeling that we would begin in earnest the next day.

Pastor Petro (Peter) came to see us and gave us a great hand of welcome. His rugged, deeply lined face was kindly and it wasn't long before we proved he had a heart of gold. We fell into bed again that night, utterly exhausted, and slept until morning. Gillian, our exemplary baby, slept too, (we scarcely knew we had her!) and David, bless him, was as good as gold.

Before breakfast was over next morning, the sick folk began to arrive. A little crowd gathered around outside the kitchen door. My first cowardly thought was, perhaps if I kept out of sight, they would go away. But on the contrary, the crowd grew steadily bigger, and with a sinking feeling at the pit of my stomach, I went out to face them.

As a nurse, I had often marvelled at the skill of our medical men back in England, who from garbled accounts and a long list of symptoms, managed to make a right diagnosis. Now, in a language that was still very foreign and expressing the weirdest kind of symptoms, I had to diagnose and prescribe treatment.

There were moments almost of panic, for I could scarcely understand anything that was said. As a matter of fact, I found sign language much more effective. I was grateful to have the basic medicines as a good standby (at least until I understood the language a little more).

Peppermint essence became the cure for many ills. A young fellow, bent almost double with abdominal pain, crying out in agony, made a remarkable recovery after taking one of my powerful peppermint concoctions; ten minutes later every bit of pain was gone.

So we took up the routine of station life, quite unaware of the magnitude of the task which faced us. In spite of the primitive mud and wattle buildings, the work was good. There was a thriving church and a school of 100 to 150 pupils. Idris became the headmaster, setting and marking examination papers and occasionally teaching a class. Disciplinary measures had to be enforced. Morals were lax and one or two of the boys had to be publicly punished and expelled before morals improved. But God honoured this stand for righteousness and we had the joy of seeing many of the schoolboys come to Christ.

Our water supply gave us a few headaches in the beginning. The nearest source was a dirty old river about a mile away, which was used by the villagers for baths, washing clothes and toilet purposes. Somehow we had to convey it to the house, then make it safe for domestic use and drinking. Empty petrol drums were used for this vital chore and a wide road cut through the bush to the banks of the river so that Idris could drive the truck there. It was a job that took several schoolboys the best part of the morning and was valuable time lost for Idris. No wonder therefore that every drop was counted precious. After Gillian had been bathed in the evening in the tin bath, David followed in the same water, then it was my turn, with Idris taking his bath last of all. Moreover such a precious commodity was not carelessly thrown away even then, but used for watering the plants.

To make this water fit to drink was quite some process. First of all we filled several buckets with water, and then sprinkled grated alum on the top. In two hours' time there was a thick sedimentation at the bottom of each bucket. The water was then boiled and poured into a filter, where it drained slowly through into the bottom container. This was now considered free from germs, but as a further precaution was boiled again. Needless to say, by this time it was flat and needed some kind of fruit juice to make it palatable.

Shortly after moving to Lulimba, Frank Holder and Idris left for a survey itinerary of the work in the Lulenge and Kabambare areas. Communications were quite impossible in the Congo. There was no delivery of mail and the nearest post office was 60 miles away. I cheerily waved them off one morning and that was the last I saw or heard of them until two weeks later when they returned.

By this time the extreme loneliness had just about reduced me to a nervous wreck, with a stomach that could not tolerate food of any description. David too was off his food, fretful and miserable, giving me many anxious moments. Thankfully the day came when the noise of a car engine was heard in the distance and what's more it was coming our way! Picking David up I ran outside, straining my eyes to catch the first glimpse — and there it was. Through the tall elephant grass the welcome sight of the Chevrolet. When at last it drew up at the door of the mission house and Idris jumped down, David's heart-rending cry of "Daddy!" eloquently revealed the secret pining of his heart. United once more, the odd symptoms disappeared, appetites were restored and everything returned to normal.

Bush fires were fascinating when seen from a distance and with the wind conveniently blowing away from one's own property, but very frightening otherwise. Towards the end of the dry season, when the grass was as dry as tinder, it needed just a spark to start a raging inferno. With so many thatched buildings on the mission station, it was imperative to "burn back" from our house, leaving us safely surrounded by charred earth.

Unfortunately and quite accidentally, this plan misfired at times and we were caught unawares. The careless throwing of a match into the bush, or a spark from a village fire some miles away, would ignite the grass and in a moment it would become a raging fire which, fanned by a strong wind, would roar along, burn down villages, leap over roads and destroy everything in its path. I can never forget the awesome sight of flames 25 to 30 ft high, advancing menacingly toward us. Running with Gillian in my arms and pushing David on ahead to what I hoped was a safe place in the clearing, I waited fearfully while Idris, the teachers and schoolboys fought to get the inferno under control.

Often the fire lay low like some somnolent fiery snake, stretching away into the distance, seemingly harmless until a sudden rising wind caused the flames to erupt to tremendous heights and to roar along like devouring monsters. One night we were awakened to the ominous sound of the crackle of flames and the acrid smell of burning. Idris leapt out of bed and disappeared into the night, leaving me alone and very afraid. The hazards of that grim fight were not known until he returned the next morning, black, dishevelled and utterly exhausted.

There was never a dull moment on the station, (what we called the area of our work) for all sorts of things were liable to break in upon the day-to-day routine. Among the many and varied needs, help for mothers in childbirth was one of the most pressing. But unfortunately, although in England I was a trained midwife, without the Antwerp Diploma I had no official backing from the Belgian Government. In the event of a maternal death, I could have been in serious trouble. I was able to give antenatal and post-natal care, as well as to save many lives in the actual deliveries, but in those earlier years, as the only nurse midwife in the area, with my hands very much tied by Government regulations, the frustration was heartbreaking.

I remember a young woman brought in by truck one evening from the Lulenge district. She was a bonny girl about 17 years of age, having been in labour for several days. There was still no sign of the baby coming. We had nowhere to put her, so she was laid on the floor of our outbuildings while I examined her. It didn't take long to diagnose an obstructed labour, with a uterus liable to rupture soon. Her only hope was a Caesarean section, but the nearest Congolese hospital was another 60 miles further on. The pain she must have suffered already, travelling over 80 miles of dirt roads, lying on the floor of the truck, was inconceivable. Before we could do anything at all to help her, her uterus ruptured and she died in 5 minutes even while she was eating some food. This had a very depressing effect on us all, a frustration which increased later, when we opened a clinic in Lulenge.

We noted how many teenage mothers died in childbirth. Some, of course, died due to disproportion (the Wabembe women had a narrow, male type of pelvis) but many of them died as a result of mishandling by the handywomen of the village and the introduction of sepsis by the witch-doctors. The native customs in the treatment of mother and new-born were so horrifying that we felt we must start something immediately to remedy this. An urgent appeal was sent to our Overseas Mission Council for midwives with the Antwerp Diploma and we set ourselves to pray for a speedy answer to this situation.

Thank God we then saw a complete reversal of this most needy section of the work. We stayed in Lulimba for 2 years and 3 months and I think, passed through every emotional crisis possible. It was to us a baptism of fire.

Following her first six months of exemplary behaviour, Gillian went through a most difficult stage, refusing to take anything other than milk. It was a battle of wills. I spare my readers the depressing details; sufficient to say that every mealtime became a nightmare, lasting at least two hours and leaving me utterly exhausted and more often than not defeated. The evening feed was particularly trying. We were tired, malarial mosquitoes buzzed around angrily and there was little comfort in sitting on an unyielding tin trunk. The nights were equally frustrating, as around 2 a.m.

Gillian would kneel up in her cot and rattle the bars until we were all wide awake, the uneven floor giving greater play to the rocking of the cot. We used all conceivable means to stop her, even tying her down, but somehow she broke free and continued to give us a rattling good time until our nerves were jangling. One can tolerate a few disturbed nights, maybe a week or two, but this went on for months until we were almost beside ourselves.

Bringing up children is not an easy task in any country. A fine social service helps considerably, but in the bush, with the nearest doctor 60 or so miles away, no telephone system and no wider family to support, toothache, earache, rashes and other minor ailments can become major anxieties. Nursing a feverish child all night or sitting by the cot side of a sick baby, wondering whether or not to make that hazardous journey to the doctor, which included the mountain escarpment, are memories that will never be erased. Nor the amazing sequel to so many of our dilemmas when, in desperation we sought the Great Physician's help, and saw miracles of healing enacted before our eyes.

The day our little boy was given back to us, seemingly from the dead, is still sharply etched upon our memories. We were staying with Swedish friends 5 miles out of town. The day before, I had come out of hospital with our new daughter, a homecoming that was somewhat dampened by the news of our 18-month-old son's nasty fall from the high bed onto a cement floor. Now, 24 hours later, he had collapsed, was cold, clammy and lifeless. We were alone in the house and had no vehicle to get us to hospital, but even as we called on God for help, a Swedish missionary (a stranger to us) drove up to the house and immediately offered his services. David was not breathing and had no pulse or heartbeat as we rushed him to Usumbura. At the hospital they said he was dead. I remember that the sister gave Coramine into the heart muscle without any response. No other medical help was available; the only doctor was out in the bush hunting. We sat by his cot in the darkened room, our hearts filled with anguish, but waiting on God for a miracle. Suddenly it happened! David opened his eyes, looked around and stood up by the cot side! Life, consciousness, and health all returned in a moment of time — an inexplicable mystery which left the hospital sister and staff mystified.

Our faith was greatly strengthened by this mighty intervention of the miraculous. God was with us, the mighty God who works wonders. We were to prove over and over again during our first term in the Congo His providential care of us, His protecting presence with us in our journeys and His miraculous provision.

Out there in the loneliness of a bush station where our nearest provision store was 150 miles away — a two-day journey over the rough, uneven dirt roads — gave us ample opportunity to prove the faithfulness of God. We had been without potatoes for several days, using rice as a substitute, until that too was in short supply. Our prayer for this need was answered by a young man from the mountains arriving on our doorstep.

"Madam," he said, "I was digging my ground a

few days ago and found these. I don't know what they are, but if you can make use of them, they are yours."

Amazingly, they were potatoes! Who had planted them up there in the wild, hilly Waruanda country we don't know, but they were located just in time to meet our need.

On another occasion, we were without meat and again brought this need to the God of supply. Sometime during the following night we were awakened by the stampeding of what sounded like a large animal, racing round and round our little hut, dragging with it something that crashed against the house and tree supports of the veranda, until we thought the walls would surely cave in. When at length the noise ceased, and Idris looked through the mosquito gauze, there, fastened by wire and stake, (part of a local trap from which it had escaped) to the centre support of the veranda, was a large antelope: three months' supply of meat. Amazing that contrary to its own instinct for survival it had rushed straight to the mission house. I could describe so many more answers to prayer like these. *"Ask and you shall receive"* is just one of the 600 or more immutable promises in the Word of God.

18

The Fight is on!

White ants — termites — were the plague of our mission station in Lulimba. The ground was infested with them. A garment accidentally dropped outside and left overnight, would disappear by the morning, with only the buttons left for identification. We were often overrun, sometimes waking up in the morning to find an ant hill of 2 ft or more beside the bed. In spite of every precaution, they invaded our trunks, playing havoc with the contents.

Very cleverly they worked, always in the dark, building themselves a small mud tunnel, through which they reached out to cupboards or chairs, or whatever object they wished to attack. Mud brick held no barrier for them; they simply ate their way through. Later on, when building our house in Lulenge, although again building in mud brick, we strongly discouraged them by laying an ant-proof course of aluminium sheeting over the second layer of bricks, overlapping the walls by 2" either side. This they found difficult to overcome. Even so, if left undisturbed for 2 or 3 days, we would find a small mud tunnel stretching from the edge of the ant-proof course out into the room, advancing relentlessly towards the furniture. In Lulimba, however, there were no such barriers. I sometimes think we must have lived on an ant hill. Lying in bed at night we would hear the "whish whish" as they energetically and ruthlessly worked their destructive way. Once or twice a year the female ants developed wings, forcing their way through the hard-baked earth in swarms, no doubt to start other termite colonies, though hundreds perished.

The local villagers loved to eat them; they had a high fat content, so they snatched them straight out of the air and into their mouths. The chickens too waited impatiently, gobbling them up greedily as they struggled through the ground, and even the birds swooped for the tasty morsels.

Walking into my bedroom one day I was startled to find it dense with flying termites. It was like walking into a thick mist, and still they were pouring up through the ground. I made a quick withdrawal, leaving them to disperse as best they could, thankful for the many gaps and openings which made a quick getaway for them possible!

So much could be said about the bird, insect and animal life of the Congo; the exotic colouring of some of the birds as they darted through the forests, weird and wonderful insects, many of them nameless to us but nevertheless creatures to be reckoned with. There was the tantalising little creature which burrowed deep into the earth just outside our bedroom window to make his home. We hardly knew he was there during the day, but in the stillness of the night he would pop up regularly, sit on the edge of the hole and sing in a high screaming tone until the entire household was wide awake. I remember one night Idris and a fellow missionary in desperation stole out, clad only in pyjamas and armed with a torch and a sizeable stick, intent on finishing his little capers once and for all. An hour later they crept desolately back into bed, absolutely thwarted. He was too quick for them. Peace and quiet only returned after one of the local boys dug him out — which was quite a job.

There was a strange insect that lived in the thatched roof, chirping noisily all night, making sleep impossible. To catch it required all the skill and patience we possessed, and more often than not it escaped us. Many a night we would wait in the darkness until quite sure we had located it then, while Idris waited with a stick poised ready to strike, I would shine the torch just as it disappeared; only to return as we were dropping off into an exhausted sleep.

Yet another creature, a wicked-looking parasite the size of a beetle, with a coat seemingly as tough as the skin of a rhinoceros, would dig his claws into one's flesh and hang on tenaciously. However, perhaps the most aggravating of our nightly visitors was the one which waited until the pressure lamp was extinguished and we were all safely settled under the mosquito net composing ourselves for sleep. Suddenly we would hear a ping, the sound of a sharp snip and something would cut through the binding at the top of the net and quite often through the tapes which held it in position, causing us to be buried beneath folds of mosquito netting. Only if you have balanced precariously on the uncertain foundation of a wire spring and Dunlopillo mattress, endeavouring in the darkness with just the light of a torch to mend a 3" rent, can you understand the intense irritation of it all. We never did catch a glimpse of this infuriating creature, but night after night, as regularly as clockwork, the net fell on top of us and yet another darn or another patch was added, to improve the appearance of our protective covering. The fight was on all right. With no ceiling for protection, we were invaded from all sides. Centipedes dropped from the thatch. An occasional snake appeared from under the bed, while one evening I caught a tree lizard the size of a young crocodile, making his way over the wall into our bedroom.

I always had a sentimental fondness for chameleons, until one day I looked down into the cold bulging eyes of one of them, as it crawled up the front of my dress. How long it had been there, I hardly dared to think. It had escaped detection by adopting, as they do, the colour of its surroundings, but all fondness disappeared like mist before the sun, when I looked down into its ugly face with the protruding eyes swivelling now and again to look behind.

I could write reams about the ant — that in-genious, industrious little insect which has cap-tured the imagination of so many writers. For ourselves, after a few painful encounters (they could all sting or bite) we learned to avoid them, carefully watching where we walked in case we stepped into a column of driver ants. And we were very particular too where we sat ... A visit from the soldier ants was something to be feared. On two occasions we did battle consistently for three days and nights before they departed. No, it was not the ferocious lion, the wild pig or even the buffalo with which we fought our hardest battle, but the constant warfare against these smaller pests, parasites and disease-producing ticks and mites. The ordinary-looking housefly and bluebottle all had a sting, as did the tsetse fly, which somehow got into the car before we could shut the windows. Surprisingly, after a few years we adapted to these conditions. We could even joke with one another as we met and exchanged experiences.

Every Christmas, for the first few years at any rate, all our missionary friends congregated at Baraka for our annual conference. They were great reunions and so much appreciated by all of us after months on lonely bush stations. Reinforcements were arriving quite regularly now; schools were being built and missionary teachers taking over. Two qualified nurses with the Antwerp Diploma were on their way and although with an ever-expanding field our business sessions grew lengthier, the outlook was most encouraging.

When our third baby, Linda Elizabeth, arrived on November 29th 1955, the Congolese called her "the smiling baby". She was indeed a treasure, happy and contented she gave us hours of pleasure. I think it was one of the happiest periods we spent at Lulimba. The work was progressing well. We were more confident with the language and Gillian was over her feeding difficulties. Linda was with us just 6 months, when quite suddenly she was stricken with something deadly, and died on the third day. Quite unexpectedly another missionary, Wesley Beardsmore, had arrived in time to travel with Idris to take our baby to see the doctor, (between 60 and 70 miles away). Returning home with a reassuring report and the baby in an apparently peaceful sleep, the two men left the next morning for a survey visit of our old Kalembe-lembe station. I was left with our sick baby, Mrs Beardsmore, who was burning with a fever, her little boy aged four and a half, and David and Gillian. Linda never seemed to come out of the deep sleep she was in, and died at 6 o'clock that evening.

Through this sad and traumatic experience God wonderfully upheld and sustained us. Rarely have I known such warmth of love and sympathy as emanated from the silent group of women who just sat in the clearing outside the door, nor the thoughtful concern of the pastor, and the courage of the teachers who willingly undertook to make that perilous journey all night, through elephant and buffalo country, to bring our men back.

They arrived at 5 o'clock in the morning. Before we left for Baraka, we read together the Daily Light portion for the day, 15th May. If you have the Daily Light, read that day's portion; it couldn't have been more appropriate. God was speaking to us in our deep grief. How wonderful His Word: *"God shall wipe away all tears ... there shall he no more death neither sorrow nor crying."* (Rev 21: 4) *"Death is swallowed up in victory."* (1 Cor 15: 54) In the fiery affliction of our deepest sorrow, He is there to strengthen and support. The day after we buried our little one, we attended a convention in one of the villages, to the amazement of the people, particularly the women. In their time of grief even the Christian women shut themselves away in a dark hut for two or three weeks, refusing to wash or eat. *"We sorrow not as those without hope"* (1 Thess 4:13) and Daniel the Pastor used the occasion to bring home this blessed truth: that the Christian's grief is not one of black despair.

The following week and back in Lulimba, we were surprised to see a jeep station wagon drive up to our door and out of it stepped three immaculately dressed American ladies: Joy Ridderhoff of Gospel Recordings with her two companions. We recognised the amazing zeal and courage that inspired and sustained these three single ladies, without knowledge of French or tribal language, to drive thousands of miles across Africa into the heart of the Congo bush land and to leave the comforts and luxuries of home for the uncertainties and hazards of such a journey.

We heard the incredible story of a young woman's vision and the adventures experienced in the fulfilling of it. Joy Ridderhoff had been invalided home after a first term of missionary service. It seemed like the end of everything for her, but God gave her a vision of encircling the globe with Gospel recordings in every known language and dialect. What a quest for a delicate girl having no financial backing, no influential friends and knowing nothing about making records, but courageously she made a start and God blessed her. Money began to pour in, voluntary helpers gave of their time, and from small beginnings there grew a work that spanned the whole world in its outreach.

Joy Ridderhoff had visited China, India, the Tibetan border and now Africa, personally supervising the recording of native languages and dialects so that the tribes could hear the Gospel in their own tongue. We counted it a privilege to help in the recording of yet a further three tribal languages and were glad to be a part of this work, seeing how patiently our friends persevered until the simple message of the Gospel was clearly outlined and understood. A parcel of 12 records, we were told, would be sent free of charge to anyone who wished to have them, together with a simple record player if they so desired. These three gracious ladies were a tremendous blessing to us, coming so soon after our grievous loss, when our arms ached to hold our baby again. It seemed they were specially sent. We rarely saw a visitor, but when anyone did come, their arrival was usually perfectly timed to meet some outstanding need. He who loves us and is touched with the feelings of our infirmities, directed His ministering servants to us on more than one occasion.

19

Breaking New Ground

With Mr and Mrs Holder now back from furlough and the Beardsmores expecting to return to their own station in Lulimba, we had been directed by the Field Council to open up a new work in the Lulenge area, some 80 miles further into the jungle. Idris, together with Wesley Beardsmore and another fellow missionary, Don Gordon, who was visiting us from the C.E.M. (Congo Evangelistic Mission) had already done a survey, marking out an admirable site for the new Mission Station. The ten hectares of ground had been granted us by the Government and we were looking forward to developing it.

Idris moved up there first, living rough in one of the villages while he worked every hour of daylight on the site. With no one to look after him, however, his health deteriorated and the result was he suffered one corneal ulcer after another on his eyes, with pain which was unbearable.

As for myself in Lulimba, the weeks stretched interminably, with a loneliness that was acute, not noticeable so much during the day, with all the many activities, but the evenings were long. Our meetings were usually over before 6 p.m. to allow the folk to get back home before darkness fell. With the children in bed and asleep an eerie silence settled on the place. My thoughts often turned then to our two gallant veteran missionaries, Misses Noad and Hegi. These two single ladies had lived alone for years, separated from one another by 100 miles or more, with no means of reaching each other except either on foot over the mountains or several hours by lake in a small dugout canoe. What lonely hours they must have endured.

Unexpectedly Idris returned at the beginning of the third week with the good news that we were moving up as a family to Lulenge. Arrangements had been made for us to live in the teacher's house in the village until our own house was completed. In a matter of days we were packed and ready, a hired truck conveying all our goods and furniture. We saw it drive off with some misgivings, piled dangerously high, with our boy Simoni perched on top and swaying with it as it rounded the bend. We wondered if it would arrive intact.

The teacher's house was situated at the far end of the village, a sturdily-built mud brick house with thatched roof. The main living room was whitewashed and boasted a ceiling! The two bedrooms, however, were mud plastered with a tiny window in each but no ceilings. I often wondered if our local villagers preferred the mud-coloured walls in order to camouflage the huge cockroaches which crawled

Ruth and Idris with David, Gillian and baby Linda.

everywhere. Once again, we were thankful for the security of mosquito nets, especially when we were visited at night by wild bush cats, which actually prowled around among the beams over our heads, and once almost overbalanced onto the children's beds. Nevertheless we soon made it home and were there for three months.

It was while we were living in such close proximity to the nationals that we heard with disturbing frequency the death wail and saw youngsters as well as adults die within a matter of hours. It seemed we were living in the midst of death and disease. Our teacher's little girl aged 12 complained of a headache one morning and by 6 p.m. that same day she was dead. No doubt it was cerebral malaria. There was little we could do. We found it all very depressing. Our children played barefoot with the children of the village, adopting many of their ways and surrounded by so much infection it was frightening. Our great comfort was the rock-firm promises of God's word: *"None of these diseases"* (Exodus 15: 26), *"no plague shall come near your dwelling"* (Psalm 91:10). Occasionally, there was a drunken orgy to keep us awake at night, the frenzied dancing and bawdy songs continuing well into the morning.

In the meantime the building of our house proceeded quite slowly. The Congolese builders would not be hurried, but with the rainy season due in just over a month's time we were working against great odds. Our efforts to try and hurry them along by carrying bricks ourselves met only with placid disdain. Fretting and fuming on our part achieved nothing.

179

The onset of the rains a month earlier than anticipated took everyone by surprise. Confined to the village with what seemed to be the worst storm ever encountered, we watched helplessly as giant trees crashed to the ground and roads became rivers in a very short time. Our concern was for the partially built house with its walls of sun-dried bricks, now exposed to the driving rain. The grass that had been laid over them for protection must have been swept away long ago. Hopefully we waited for the storm to pass, but relentlessly the rain continued until the village was a sea of mud with no possibility of moving the truck from where it was now, completely bogged down.

When the fourth day dawned to still leaden skies and heavy rain, we gave up hope. I think it was then that we touched the bottom of despair. Only God could save the situation and our faith was so abysmally low just then that we couldn't see what God could do either. Kneeling there, with everything collapsing around us, we put up our puny ultimatum: that if the walls were destroyed we would return home.

During the 50 or so years of my Christian pilgrimage I have come to know something of the longsuffering nature of God and His unwearying patience with our smallness and pitiable doubts. When at last we drove around to see the house, it was to find the walls not only standing, but hardly damaged at all! A miracle indeed! Just a few rounded corners to remind us of the test of faith and our dismal failure. What's more, we moved into it in record time, despite repeated storms, for the rainy season was indeed upon us.

How thrilled we were to have such a lovely place to live in. One of our churches at home had designated a gift towards cement for the floors and glass for the windows, so we were moving into a semi-permanent house. The novelty of two doors fascinated the children, who raced in one and out of the other until they, as well as the rest of us, were dizzy. The security of a ceiling, windows to shut at night and a solid concrete floor, all combined to make life much easier and gave us a home of which we were proud.

The Mission Station was pleasantly situated; its elevated position gave us a wide panoramic view of the countryside with its ranges of mountains in the near distance.

The forest area reminded us of Tarzan of the Apes country with its wild vines and creepers, giant trees and exotic birds. We thought to cultivate a picnic area there for the children, perhaps dam up the river for bathing purposes, but gave up the idea when we found the place alive with snakes and other wildlife. We did, however, find the warm moist soil ideal for banana groves and the growing of sugar cane. Our vegetable garden too was proving a great success.

The prospects seemed rosy. Idris's day school was functioning well, with more and more boys being added. Every available piece of wood was utilised for desks. A temporary church had been erected and was already too small to house the people. Our two pastors, Eliya Yuma and Paulo Isa, were giants in spiritual stature, utterly devoted to the cause of Christ.

They told us the thrilling story of how the work

began in Lulenge.   Only 17 years previously, cannibalism was practised in the area and such degrees of idolatry and witchcraft that made the spine tingle — a stronghold of Satan indeed.   Then Eliya who, while serving as kitchen boy for Mr and Mrs Buck, (former missionaries) came to know Jesus as Saviour, and hearing the unmistakable call of God to go and evangelise among his own countrymen, he moved into this vast, formidable territory.

Paulo Isa had the same calling, and together they ventured for Christ, opening up the entire area to the Gospel. Eliya told us something of the hatred and persecution they had to endure as they moved from village to village preaching the word, and as they baptised new converts and established churches.

The witchdoctors pronounced curses over them, their food was poisoned and often they barely escaped with their lives, yet they proved over and over again that in Christ, the power of the witch-doctor is smashed and the bonds of superstition broken.   One wonderful testimony of God's divine intervention was the occasion when the witch-doctor, incensed against a young Christian worker because of his apparent success, had, through sorcery, called a lion from the bush to devour him. Eliya told us that the lion actually came into the village, wandered into the open doorway of the hut where the young man lay asleep, squatted on its haunches and then slept too, returning to the bush later, without harming a hair of his head.   They experienced miraculous deliverance, but also great suffering.   Eliya told us how he lost his entire family in one week as a result of poisoning. But later God had given him another family: a wife and three sturdy little boys, now growing into young manhood. So to a large extent, we entered into their labours and by the grace of God, were able to see further fantastic growth of the church of Jesus Christ in and around Lulenge.

What marvellous trophies of grace there were. Michael Bunduki, for instance, was a renowned witchdoctor, so diabolically clever with his evil enchantments that everyone stood in awe of him. He could call elephants at will, and exercised this demonic power over the animals until, as well as being a famous witchdoctor, he made a name for himself as a great hunter.

God wanted this man for himself, so that he would be set free from demonic control and learn to love. And so began a series of calamitous events in which he completely lost confidence in himself. He was almost killed by one of the elephants which he usually dominated, and God by His Spirit brought this man to his knees, crying for mercy. His life was transformed.

News was brought to us one day that the great Paramount Chief of the Warega tribe and his retinue were on their way to see us. We had heard of this man, and knew something of the power he wielded. He could be fierce in his anger when opposed, so that people feared him. He was also very antagonistic to the Christian Gospel and had refused us permission to preach in his area. With some trepidation therefore, we waited for his arrival. The village had been swept clean, work was suspended and everyone hung nervously around, waiting. When at last the Chief and his people arrived and crowded into our little room, we had the best chair reserved for him, a cup of tea ready and cakes made just that morning. Thank God I was able, with aspirin, to dispel a nasty headache from which he was suffering, so that before he left he was completely won over, inviting us into his country to preach whenever we cared to go.

The amazing sequel to this event is that some time later Geoff Hawksley, who took over the Makombo station while we were on furlough, had the joy of seeing a mighty revival-type move of God break out among the Warega and hundreds were won to the Lord.

Although we were completely isolated from other missionary friends, and stationed a distance of three days' journey from the nearest township of Usumbura (now Bujumbura), where we purchased stores and medical supplies, we were very happy in Lulenge.

From virgin forest, a lovely mission station was slowly emerging. A variety of fruit trees and many graceful palms added their beauty, whilst quick-growing trees with their scented yellow flowers lined a wide road which led from the house to the school building and church and encircled the entire station. Bricks were now in the process of being made for a new permanent church building. A little house was being erected for Pauline Bagshaw, our missionary nurse, who was expected in the near future, and plans had been finalised for a maternity hospital. Every six months we made a trip to our nearest shopping centre, returning so heavily

David and Gillian in the long grass with some Congolese

loaded that the 60-minute part of the 60-mile journey, over the Lulimba escarpment in particular, became a dreaded hazard — especially if undertaken during the rainy season. I could write at length of God's care and protection during those hazardous journeys. The appalling skids and almost certain death, from which we were miraculously delivered, showed us that truly the angels of God encamped round about us and the whole route from Lulenge to Baraka was marked to us for ever by singular evidences of His protection.

I remember the lonely forest road, where with our two little ones we had spent a long night waiting for Mr Holder to come and tow us into Lulimba, our boy working non-stop to feed a blazing fire and so keeping marauding animals at bay.

Then there was the spot where our vehicle left the road in a bad skid, shot down a steep embankment and miraculously, before it could become embedded in the thick mud swamp, bounced back on to the road again! I remember the hair-raising experiences negotiating the various bridges when, with tyres caked with mud, the truck veered steadily towards the unguarded edge, and only the mercy of God saved us from shooting over into the swirling waters beneath.

All these harrowing experiences left an indelible mark on my heart and mind; and the frailty of my faith made me all too vulnerable, with the result that I passed through a period of great darkness, when it seemed my nervous system couldn't take any more. Idris at this time developed what appeared to be arthritis, and he became immobile.

Anxiously we waited for the doctor to make his

bi-monthly visit to the local people's dispensary in the village. The treatment he prescribed was a course of cortisone tablets (so far unknown to me at the time) that produced such terrible side-effects that I thought he would die. Once again we were thrown back on God, who graciously restored him to health and strength.

Shortly after this, however, I suffered acute abdominal pain, which in my nervous state opened me up to Satan's suggestion that it might well be a malignant growth. My heart was filled with fear. I know that I was not far from a complete nervous breakdown, but thank God for a partner who prayed daily with me and read passages from the Word of God that inspired faith and courage. Even so there were weeks and months of such darkness and desolation known only to God when, instead of faith there was a gripping fear. The pain continued, and eventually I had to submit to surgery. Yet out of this experience I learned the faithfulness and comfort of the Lord.

Our next patient was Gillian, who became dreadfully ill. She was unable to take even milk without vomiting, and her little face was so pathetically white and drawn that the Chef-de-poste, visiting us one day, expressed his alarm and concern at the state of her health. But we had another wonderful answer to prayer when my mother, not knowing what was happening to Gillian, was moved to put into a parcel a tin of Bengers Food, (a milk preparation for invalids) which arrived at this very time of need, and was tolerated without vomiting. It thus brought healing and life to Gillian again.

The years had taken their toll; the heat, fever, the inroads of ill health, and the loneliness, had all combined to sap vitality, bringing us near to breaking point. Now it seemed that every molehill appeared as a mountain, and our long-awaited furlough seemed so far away in the future. We were also haunted by secret fears that we would never see England again.

20

Unpredictable Days

The time for furlough did eventually arrive, and in February 1958 we were on our way. Fears and misgivings dispersed as the ship carried us daily nearer home. For the children an exciting new life began as they discovered water on tap, electric lights, flush toilets, and all the wonders and mysteries aboard. Then at last London's familiar red buses; friendly policemen; tube trains; cockney brogue and neon lights — an exciting prelude to reunion with friends, loved ones, home, rest and relaxation. Slowly, the past receded; taut nerves healed; the future again became full of promises; what's more, we were able to look back with unclouded vision and rejoice at what God had done.

Mother bustled about in her usual brisk manner. She was now 74 years of age and as well and keen as ever. The family, apart from my younger brother Arthur (now married and living in New Zealand), was complete. Stanley, my eldest brother, was home from the United States, and the garden of 17 The Crescent rang with happy laughter.

The months passed. Dr Priddy of the Swansea Bible College kindly took David and Gillian as boarders into the Missionary Home of Emmanuel Grammar School, while Idris and I itinerated around the Assemblies. Idris's health was poor, and though I was able to relieve him considerably in ministry, we both realised there was a definite need of healing for his body. There were so many needs to be met before we could return to the field.

A new vehicle was a must, as were complete outfits and passage money for the four of us, all estimated to require at least £3,000; a formidable sum in those days. The amazing ways in which these needs were met, strengthened our faith and built a greater confidence in Him who was undoubtedly preparing the way. How thrilled we were when the Youth Council launched a "Speed the Light"' project for a vehicle, so that when we left England, we were in possession of a new Land Rover provided by the donations. We praised God too that Idris had received a mighty touch of healing and was rejoicing in renewed health.

Re-commissioned and re-equipped, we set sail on the Durban Castle once more, on Friday 13th November 1959 on what was to be the most eventful period of our missionary service. The journey itself was full of incident. We sailed through an un-usually vicious storm in the Mediterranean; our trailer was unfortunately misplaced when the ship unloaded at Mombasa, and our fellow missionary who was coming to work with us, Miss Evelyn Thomas, discovered that her luggage had been reloaded onto the wrong ship and sent down the coast. All this caused considerable delay, so that some W.E.C. missionary friends, with whom we were to travel overland, were obliged to move off without us. This meant that Evelyn had to drive for the first time her brand-new Land Rover (also provided through donations) over unknown and uncertain terrain.

It was our second day's journey from Nairobi to Uganda. We were leading the way and Evelyn was following. We became aware that she was not behind us. Retracing our journey we found her. She had been involved in a serious accident — her Land Rover had left the road, had somersaulted twice, throwing her through the open steel top into the bush. Evelyn was picked up for dead. But God graciously undertook and some days later Evelyn was pronounced out of danger.

So we were able to proceed on our way, leaving her in the capable hands of British doctors and nurses in the hospital at Kampala. For two more days we drove through spectacular and beautiful country, over mountain escarpments, through heavily wooded forests and around numerous narrow, hairpin bends, until we found ourselves dropping into Bujumbura via the Astrida Road.

Thick clouds like fog obscured our vision. Inching our way over the mountain passes, with deep gorges on either side, became a terrifying nightmare from which we thankfully emerged some four hours later, when we dropped into the town and realised our journey was almost at an end ... On familiar ground once more, we were soon making our way to Baraka, and by nightfall were renewing fellowship with Frank and Ivy Holder.

Early next morning, with the prospect of a clear day, we set off on the final lap of our journey to Lulenge. In the security of our new vehicle, the treacherous bridges and bad spots on the road were negotiated without a hitch, and in record time we were rolling into Makombo, to the shouts of welcome from our village Christians. We were also welcomed by Geoff and Brenda Hawksley, who had so capably taken care of the work during our absence.

It was only two days before Christmas, and the New Year would see us on safari again, taking our children, who had flown out to us from boarding school in Wales, to school in Rhodesia. In the meantime there was our great Christmas Convention — busy happy days of fellowship with nearly 2,000 of our African believers.

In the house, Brenda and I muddled through from one day to the next, packing and unpacking. There were little garments to sort out and mark; half-empty boxes littered the place; a mounting pile of dirty washing harassed us, and then in the midst of it all, Gillian went down with a bad attack of malaria. The scheduled date of departure saw us ready, nevertheless. Miraculously, in answer to prayer, Gillian's temperature dropped to normal once again, and we were on the road, sharing adventures this time with Geoff and Brenda Hawksley, whose daughter Ruth would be attending the same Government school as our own children.

Much could be written of this trip. We had the

joy of meeting up with old friends not seen for years at the various Z.E.M. stations en route. I remember the sheer panic of feeling the Land Rover out of control in some of the worst skids ever. David became very ill on the second day of our journey and his temperature soared to 105.6° F. We were so grateful for the loving concern of Fred and Isobel Ramsbottom at the Katompe station, where we stayed for several days, and I appreciated the relief of sharing the anxiety with Miss Ralphs and Miss Barnes, our two missionary nurses there.

Some seven or eight days later, we crossed the Congo border and proceeded into Northern Rhodesia (now Zambia). The children were to be boarded out with a young Christian lady in Chingola, a small town on the copper belt, 15 miles from the Congo border. We found her modest, two - bedroomed flat with little difficulty and marvelled that she successfully accommodated our party of eight as well as her own family of four.

The next three days sped by in a feverish rush of shopping, buying school uniforms, and attending interviews. David's poor state of health caused us much concern, for his blood count was dangerously low. The tender years of our little girl and the prospect of leaving her tugged at our heart strings, making us turn once again to Him who had made the supreme sacrifice. We were not entrusting our little ones to strangers, but just committing them to Him who had lent them to us in the beginning. They were not to be the victims of our consecration, for He is Lord and we were content to leave them in His care.

The return journey was not without its hazards.

There were moments of real danger. But once we were safely back in Makombo we thanked God for preserving mercies. 18 days on the road in the height of the rainy season had been extremely wearing. Little did we know that this was to be the pattern of things during the next months — that we were to travel more during this short term than ever before, and our safety would depend to a large extent upon this dependable vehicle.

Station life very soon absorbed us. We had returned with plans for a new maternity hospital as well as a new mission home. Pauline Bagshaw was now in charge of flourishing maternity work and life was never dull. With no available doctor we tackled all kinds of abnormalities, and by God's help, saved mothers' lives, if not always the babies'. In the face of so much abysmal ignorance and witchdoctor interference, mothers came to us in moribund (approaching death) condition, with highly septic abdomens, almost beyond our help. Pauline, in order to save her sanity, had been obliged to adopt a Congolese kind of psychology that was to preach the Gospel to them, pray for them, and then do what she could. The results were often amazing. With the women often having an elongated pelvis, there were many obstructed labours and hard births. Good antenatal care reduced this hazard a little, but we continually faced the pressure and strains of midwifery problems quite outside our province. Furthermore, this high drama was acted out in a mud and wattle hut with a limited supply of water and drugs and the minimum of furniture and instruments.

The days sped by. The station was a beehive of

activity from morning until night, and girls' and women's classes were now a popular feature, extending our evangelical outreach. Meetings were held morning and evening in the hospital, and the maternity ward became a marvellous sounding board for the Gospel. As entire families accompanied the patient, our congregations were already made. The clinics too had their Gospel Service. With a hundred and more babies in for weighing and treatment, it meant we had a congregation of at least a hundred mothers to hear the news of Salvation. We were so happy with these wonderful opportunities that we almost resented the interruption when together with our Congolese pastors we had to make another trip to Baraka for our annual conference. This time we were saddened to note the changing attitude of some of the Congolese pastors and teachers. There was mistrust and suspicion.

Uhura (independence) filled their minds and warped their thinking; fellowship was strained and we returned to our stations with serious misgivings concerning the future and a sense of inadequacy to meet the materialism that was creeping into the church. This awareness increased during the following weeks and deepened into a burden from which we only found relief as we gave ourselves to prayer and intercession for our African brethren. Night after night we sought the Lord's face for the intervention of His Spirit in an increasingly hardening situation.

The answer to our prayers came quite unexpectedly one Sunday morning some four or five weeks later. We were sitting quietly meditating for a few minutes, following our communion service, before making our way home. The ministered word had stirred our hearts and no one seemed inclined to move. There was, in fact, a quiet air of expectancy as we waited in the presence of God.

Suddenly it happened. The power of God filled the place, with a resultant, sudden eruption of praise and worship as the Holy Spirit touched one after another. Simple village women spoke in tongues while others interpreted. There was prophecy and singing in the Spirit with waves of power and glory, transforming that small bamboo hut into a veritable gate of heaven. Imagine a poor ignorant village woman who only spoke the local Kilembe, praising the Lord in the purest English! The burden of the message, whether by tongue or interpretation or by prophecy, was the same, namely that a great darkness was coming on the land and the people were exhorted to draw near to God. Pastor Paulo, sitting at the front, had looked on in bewilderment for a few minutes then, thinking everyone was a little out of order, made several attempts to sing them down with a chorus, but was himself carried away likewise and borne along in the Holy Spirit. It is a fact that at his feet, at the close of the service, there was a pool of water that was his tears. What a change there was now in the attitude of the people. The suspicion was gone; instead we were united in a wonderful love.

This was the beginning of a gracious move of the Spirit of God. The blessing swept right through the villages as my husband, together with two African pastors, travelled around the area ministering the Word and praying for believers to be filled with the Holy Spirit. In the light of future catastrophic happenings in the land, we can only thank God that in His mercy He visited the people, preparing them for the future events. We continued to enjoy wonderful visitations from God with outpourings of His Spirit, until it culminated in a great Whitsuntide convention among the Warundi people. In one meeting alone 120 of these mountain folk were filled with the Holy Spirit. So great was the power of God among us that the thousand or more believers danced with sheer joy, and their praise echoed and re-echoed around the mountains.

During this time we travelled into the mountains to visit the remote villages. These were wonderful, holy days of fellowship, well worth the pain and weariness of that long safari. This involved climbing 10,000 feet, then dropping to sheer-sided river beds; crossing weird and wonderful bridges; wading through evil-smelling swamps; being carried on the back of one of our Congolese brethren over swift-flowing rivers; the blazing sun and intense thirst; the sunburn sores that took months to heal; aching legs and gasping breath. Yes, it was well worth the suffering and hardship for the joy of sharing with our African Christians such heights of blessing. Dropping down to the torrid heat of the plains and the close confines of the valley villages with their rats, mosquitoes and cockroaches, was somewhat of an anticlimax (the cold air of the mountains had kept such pests at bay) but Heaven's breezes continued to blow and there was a sweet breath of the Spirit of God as we ministered around the churches.

We arrived back at Makombo just two weeks before Independence. Our little house looked like a palace and soon we were enjoying the delights of a hot bath and quenching our thirst with copious drinks of ice-cold water from the fridge. Uhura was on everyone's lips. We sensed a mounting excitement as the day of independence drew near. June 30th was the due day and we wondered what it would bring! Unfortunately to some of the country folk, it spelled freedom to help themselves to anyone's goods. To others who had seen the white man obtain money by passing a slip of paper over a bank counter, it meant a cheque book with the possibilities of unlimited wealth. Any attempts to disillusion them met with disdain.

The Belgian Government officials were packing their treasures and moving to safer areas. Our schoolboys had already gone to their homes, leaving the ripe cotton for us missionaries to harvest if we wanted to sell it. The station was oppressively quiet with an air of suspense, rather like the calm before the storm.

Our contact with the outside world, should there be trouble, was to be by plane, which was to fly over the area twice daily. We were told the two pre-set signals that we were to use. We were to lay two lengths of white linen forming a cross in the event of trouble, or set it out in two parallel lines if all was well. The actual day of independence passed uneventfully. We spent it quietly on our own compound; but as the days passed we heard rumours of unrest, of rebellion among the soldiers, and of killings and terrible atrocities, particularly in the cities and townships. We ourselves were reasonably safe in Makombo, where we were well known and loved among the non-Christians as well as the Christians. We didn't expect that we would need to leave.

However, one Saturday evening, just nine days following Independence, a young Belgian drove up to the house in great haste at about 8 p.m.

"You must get out immediately," he said, "there has been an uprising not far away and the road to safety will soon be closed."

Hurriedly we packed a few clothes and a bit of food. We turned the key on all our lovely furnishings and were soon on our way. 50 miles away, we turned into the grounds of the Cotton Co., where we found a group of Belgians from many of the surrounding districts, including the two Roman Catholic priests from our own area. Each man was well armed and seemed highly overwrought. There was such a strained atmosphere that we thought the use of firearms was highly possible.

We decided to continue our journey as far as Lulimba. It was a still night. A bright moon shone through the scudding clouds, lighting our way. Hardly a ripple of wind disturbed the trees of the jungle which closed in around us. It seemed unreal that the calm of this land was already being shattered by disturbing elements, so that we were actually fleeing for our lives, leaving all possessions behind. We arrived at Lulimba at 2:30 a.m. without incident and were relieved to find Mr and Mrs Hawksley with Evelyn Thomas still there. They had waited, knowing our only way out was via their station. Despite the late hour, excitement had driven sleep from our eyes and we talked until the bell summoned us to morning service.

Later in the day, listening to the 1 p.m. news, we heard of serious trouble in Albertville: shootings and killings; white people fleeing the country and rebel soldiers advancing along the very road which led from Albertville to Lulimba. We decided it was healthier for all of us to make our way to Baraka, and left at 4 o'clock that afternoon. I can't adequately describe the perils of that journey as we cautiously drove over the Lulimba escarpment in gathering darkness, with Geoff's vehicle hardly roadworthy behind us and more difficult roads ahead.

We could hear above us the incessant droning of the planes carrying Europeans to safety; a most unusual sound in that particular mountainous area. Every now and then a car overtook us, flashing by heavily laden with refugees rushing to safety. We led the way in the Land Rover, keeping an eye through the wing mirror on what we thought were the headlights of Geoff's vehicle. Imagine then our consternation when one of the passing cars pulled in front and the driver informed us that Geoff's truck was broken down some miles behind. Knowing of the advancing soldiers it was against all natural instincts to drive back mile after mile to where Geoff's truck was stationary. Unable to repair it, we linked the two vehicles with an inadequate tow rope, and as the headlights were gone too, it became necessary for Evelyn to hold a lighted torch outside the cab, thereby giving us some indication that they were still on tow.

Our progress was painfully slow as we gingerly crawled around dangerous bends and negotiated steep hills. The tow rope broke every now and then and in mending it, it gradually became shorter until we were less than 2 ft apart, making the descent of the Fizi escarpment hazardous in the extreme...

It was with tremendous relief and thanksgiving to God that we turned in at Baraka in the early hours of the morning. The situation continued to be unpredictable. The news varied from day to day, sometimes grim, causing us to wonder if we would get out in time. Other days it was brighter and we talked of a ten-year policy of withdrawal.

In spite of this uncertainty, however, four days after our midnight flight to Baraka, we were on our return journey to Lulenge, with the Hawksleys and Evelyn Thomas accompanying us as far as Lulimba.

How delightful it was to be back. We were welcomed with open arms. Life seemed quite normal this side of the mountain, and soon we were in the throes of work once more.

21

"Like an eagle that stirs up its nest"

During the next few weeks, we tried to apply ourselves to the exciting and growing work of the station, but there were tensions. We did not have peace of mind and heart — a prerequisite for the efficient running of such a busy station. The news fluctuated daily. Diplomatic headlines were startling, with Russia threatening war unless Belgian forces withdrew, and America making tentative suggestions of financing and developing the country over a fifty-year period.

Congo was seething with political unrest. There were rebel uprisings, killings and murders, giving us moments of real fear, particularly on hearing that hospitals in the townships were full of white women who had been raped by the Congolese. Pauline's radio was our only link with the outside world, and one day, while listening to the short-wave transmitting station, we heard that other mission boards were planning full-scale evacuation. This naturally left us in a turmoil of indecision. Events followed swiftly. Some of our missionaries were already on their way to Britain, others had moved to safer areas outside Congo; we ourselves were on the road again by July 10th.

In the mercy of God we reached Albertville (Kalemia) safely. Our usual route to Baraka and Usumbura (Bujumbura) was now closed, with barriers erected. Europeans attempting to drive that way were beaten up and robbed. It was with thankful hearts therefore that we, together with the Hawksleys and Evelyn Thomas, got out before barriers were erected on this our only road to safety. Our stay of a few days in Kalemia was quite enjoyable, though we slept rough: the ladies bedding down in what had been the garage of the mission house. The steamy heat of the bush land was less pronounced here. Nights were cool, and once we were accustomed to the heavy tread of soldiers' boots and the noise of armoured vehicles throughout the night, we slept well, awaking refreshed each morning. Furthermore we were able to buy bread and fresh vegetables — an innovation which meant our health improved. The rapidly deteriorating situation, however, forced us to move again, and on August 10th we crossed Lake Tanganyika by steamer to Bujumbura and safety.

Our missionary personnel were now complete with the exception of Geoff Hawksley and Idris, who were attempting to return to Lulimba and Makombo to assess the situation. We talked late into the night, trying to form some policy for the future. Frank Holder said Baraka was calm, the road clear of barriers. Should we go back? Reluctant to admit defeat, we unanimously agreed to travel back to Baraka the next day. Our journey was uneventful and pleasant except for the catcalls and occasional shouts of "Go home to your own country!" Some waved cheerily as we passed. Little did we know that our next journey along this route would be under the care and protection of United Nations forces.

The mission houses were a shambles, but we soon brought some semblance of order. Geoff and Idris joined us on the second day, so we were together for a delayed and necessary conference with our African brethren. We were there just six weeks.

It was soon apparent that the spirit abroad in the country had now pervaded much of the Church. They wanted our money, houses, vehicles, even the mission boat, but not us.

We were dismayed at the callous attitude shown and their mistrust and lack of confidence in us. We were sick at heart. Our words were like hot air for them. The last day of the conference was worse than we feared. The ultimatum presented to us was quite unacceptable and we were left with no alternative but to withdraw from the field.

Our request for a road pass was blankly refused by the African officials; what was worse, we found we were virtually prisoners in our own compound.

Our only hope of getting out of Congo now was under escort by United Nations troops stationed in Bukavu, some 80 miles away. We were surrounded by hostile Congolese. The weather was unbearably hot. Food supplies were running low. Our nerves were taut, and tension was mounting. That evening we met together to pray that God would direct the United Nations forces our way. Mkuku, where the station was situated, was two to three miles from Baraka off the Fizi road. The mission complex, three-quarters of a mile inland from the road towards the great Tanganyika Lake, could be invisible to passers-by. Our exact location, however, was known to God. He had everything under His wonderful control.

The next morning surprisingly (?) two jeeploads of UN soldiers passed by on their way to settle some political trouble in Fizi. Mr Holder was able to intercept them, telling them of our plight. Even so there were still anxious moments, especially when the soldiers sent to protect us until we could be rescued were ordered back to camp and Mr Holder given half an hour to get them on their way. We begged the Africans to allow the single ladies and those with children to accompany them. This was granted, albeit reluctantly, and they were only allowed to take handbags with them.

Brenda Hawksley and I were left to look after the menfolk. We waved the ladies and children off with heavy hearts. When would we see them again? During the whole of these proceedings Congolese soldiers stationed themselves around the place with guns at the ready, watching our every move. The hostility was frightening; they glared at us with hatred in their eyes. What had begun as rebellion against their seeming oppressors, the Belgians, had developed into hatred of every white face, which was rapidly becoming a blood lust.

It was a tremendous relief when eventually they

piled into their truck and drove off, leaving us with an uneasy peace. Following our evening meal we sat around talking or trying to read, all without success; strange sounds made us jump and every nerve was quivering. Our vehicles were loaded ready for an emergency flight; but it was imperative that the Africans didn't learn of this. The blazing headlights of several vehicles into the drive around 8 p.m. startled us into an awareness of our position and we wondered who this was arriving. How vulnerable we were as foreigners in this unstable, unhappy land.

It was with heartfelt relief that we realised it was Frank Holder arriving with three jeeploads of United Nations troops, including the Commander and a Swedish interpreter. The troops were mainly composed of Irish lads with their ready wit and high spirits, and they were just the company we needed after the gruelling experiences of the past weeks: we felt liberated already. From their iron rations Brenda and I made them a good supper before we tumbled into bed at 11:30 p.m. The men slept on the floor where they could. Plans were to move off as early as possible the next day. The following morning as dawn broke over the Congo bush land, we were making final preparations for our journey. 5.30 a.m. saw us feeding the troops. Twenty-one men sat down for breakfast; we were glad we didn't have this chore every day! At 8.30 a.m. we moved off, an impressive convoy headed by the Commander and interpreter in a Volkswagen, the missionary vehicles following, each with an armed soldier aboard and each of our vehicles interspersed with army jeeps.

A nasty incident reminded us that we were not yet out of danger. As we drove out of Baraka a truckload of Congolese soldiers intercepted our convoy, forbidding us to proceed. Two of the United Nations soldiers, Africans who spoke the dialect, negotiated with them; and with the knowledge that another UN soldier had a sten gun levelled at them, they were finally persuaded to allow us to pass.

Three hours later we were skirting the lake, driving on a narrow road with precipitous mountains to the left; a very beautiful part of the journey. Suddenly we were engulfed in noise and confusion as boulders crashed down onto the road, narrowly missing some of the vehicles. Friction caused bushes and trees to ignite until the hillsides were ablaze. Our Land Rover pitched and tossed like a ship on a rough sea. Only when the road gaped open in front of us did we realise we were in the midst of a violent earthquake. Looking back on this frightening experience, I marvel that we came through unscathed!

We drove mile after mile with what would appear to be all hell let loose around us; the road heaving beneath us, rocks and boulders repeatedly crashing down onto the road. Once or twice the entire convoy was brought to a halt while the men struggled to move a larger boulder out of the way. We passed villages where every hut was flattened; the locals lying prostrate on the ground, terrified beyond description. Amazingly, apart from one of the soldiers who was hit by a piece of rock, we came through without injury. God's merciful care was surely ours that day.

The Swedish mission, Uvira, where we planned to

stay overnight, was in disarray and confusion. The missionaries wandered around the grounds dazed and shocked, their homes uninhabitable; the guest house damaged beyond repair. Our troubles even then were not yet over. Arriving at the Congo border, tired and hungry and indescribably dirty, we met up with aggressive, angry soldiers who demanded all our money. Only after much argument did they allow us through.

We spent the night in the Danish Baptist Mission; Brenda Hawksley and I in the house and the men in the boys' dormitory. A violent storm and a nasty earthquake aftershock robbed us of sleep or rest. Bujumbura, the then capital of Rwanda-Burundi, was a fair-sized township with quite a large population. It boasted several good stores and one or two decent hotels. At that time it was bulging at the seams with refugees and all accommodation was taken.

We eventually found a large old house in the native quarter used as a warehouse to store aeroplane parts. The owner kindly let us have it rent free provided we cleared out all the machinery. With bits of furniture loaned us by missionary friends and as many beds as we required from the Danish Mission School, the accommodation was made habitable for six of our families. Here we stayed for two months. It was certainly not the acme of comfort. We were tormented by mosquitoes, and pestered by thieves. Earth tremors continued daily for several weeks. The seismologists recorded 150 in the first twenty-four hours following the quake. Apparently we had travelled over the epicentre of the quake on that fateful day and but for the mercy of God we would have been killed.

The novelty of this nomadic existence, now in the third month, was wearing thin. We all found the situation demoralising, affecting our health and temper. Our attempts to cope with the heat, noise and lack of ordinary home comforts touched the hearts of our good friends Mr and Mrs Hollyer, ex-Congo missionaries who were now living in Bujumbura. They placed at our disposal bathing and laundry facilities in their lovely home; and a daily supply of ice cubes made drinks more palatable. Sundays became a wonderful treat; high tea with scrumptious little savouries such as caviar, crab and salmon. The recollection of these, even after twenty years, makes my mouth water.

Later we enjoyed precious fellowship as we broke bread together, returning afterwards refreshed and encouraged to our temporary and sordid surroundings. How temporary this accommodation was to be we didn't know at the time. The news was bad and there were reports of terrible atrocities, mainly, it was said, by the Baluba tribe. We were told that they had descended into a primitive savagery, hacking, torturing and killing Europeans. This lessened any hope of getting back to our stations.

Mr Woodford, our missionary secretary, came out from England with proposals from our Overseas Missionary Council, and we were in conference together for several days. A specially arranged meeting with our African pastors proved a disaster. They would not cooperate and stubbornly resisted any overtures from us.

Within days a final decision from the field led to

the sad disbanding of missionary personnel; some to go home, others to be loaned out to our Swedish friends and two couples to remain in Bujumbura for any possible negotiation with our African brethren. Idris and I were to join our children in Rhodesia (Zambia) and await events there.

Affairs were quickly wound up and on November 23rd we were on safari again, travelling this time through Tanganyika to avoid the troubled areas of Congo. Four days later, after a number of harrowing experiences on the road, we drove into Chingola to a wonderful reunion. What a joy to be with the children again after six months of disturbing experiences and fears! Mother had written to them regularly from England but there were long periods when she too had little or no news of us to pass on to them. How frightening for our children aged only 8 and 7, to hear and see Europeans fleeing to safety, passing through Chingola in battered, bullet-riddled cars; to hear about women crazed with grief having seen their husbands and children shot down by the roadside in ambush by Congolese youths, and not to know what was happening to their own parents.

We thank God that He had preserved us as a family. We were together again, enjoying every precious minute. The priority now was to find somewhere to live. Mrs Collins, who had been looking after our children, provided temporary accommodation: her family of four in one bedroom and we four in another. We were very grateful for her kindness in enduring cramped quarters with us until something else could be found. There was every possibility we could get a mine house.

Chingola was on the copper belt. Mine workers often vacated their homes for three months of the year as they moved to South Africa for holidays. Europeans were welcome as caretakers, as thieving was rife and empty houses vulnerable. A week later we moved into one of them — a luxury bungalow complete with all modern conveniences; fridge; washing machine; beautiful bedding and crockery, all we needed, and a gardener thrown in for good measure. This again was God's provision for the present need; in fact until we left for England in March of the following year we lived, as did other Congo missionaries, in mine houses at no expense to ourselves. Here we spent Christmas together as a family, delighting in the comfort of our surroundings and enjoying tranquillity after the storm. Life went on uneventfully for several weeks.

We enjoyed living in Chingola. The shops were wonderful, the climate was pleasant and Idris was soon engaged in ministry. Life seemed a lovely dream after the harrowing experiences of past months.

One day while out shopping, a placard caught our attention. It bore the startling news of the murder of two white missionaries by the Congolese. Quickly buying a newspaper, we read of the tragic deaths of our beloved Teddy Hodgson and Elton Knauf. The news stunned us. Teddy was from my home Church in Preston; we had been young people together. For years he had worked in the Congo and was greatly loved.

Shaken to the core, we seriously wondered if our work in Congo was finished. If a man who was so loved could be killed in such a barbaric way there was little hope for the rest of us. As our stay in Chingola lengthened into three months without receiving any word of hope from our friends in Bujumbura, we came to the sad conclusion that we must go home, probably never to return.

Our feelings were mixed as we boarded the plane in Ndola at the end of March 1961. Another era of our lives was ending; an exciting, adventurous, often frightening and sometimes baffling period. We were left wondering what the future would hold. England was our destination now; reunited with the family, back into the ease of our own language and to comparative calm after the storm.

We couldn't know or even imagine that there would be yet tremendously exciting, wonderful years, both at home and overseas. Little did we know at that time, when it seemed our period of useful service was over, that God would give us the joy and privilege of serving Him in pastoring various churches in the homeland and even returning to Africa to serve Him in our Nairobi Bible College. Nor could we see (for God kindly veils our eyes) the frustration and disability; after-effects of a number of strokes, that were to leave Idris with restricted mobility and obliged to rest.

As I sit in our little home, (miraculously provided) penning these last few pages of my story, my thoughts linger on the wonderful faithfulness of God. Yes, Idris sits here in his chair, almost immobile. Our missionary and pastoral work was terminated earlier than we would have planned, yet there wells up within my heart a deep thankfulness to God, who has so graciously led us through the kaleidoscope of missionary life; who has guided us over the years, provided and protected us through all the vicissitudes of experience and brought us by His grace to this present moment of time. Whatever the future holds, I will meet it with joy, knowing that I will see, as in past years, woven throughout the fabric of my life the unfolding design of His perfect will, the ultimate consummation of His divine appointment.